The FAIRIES A to Z Coloring Book

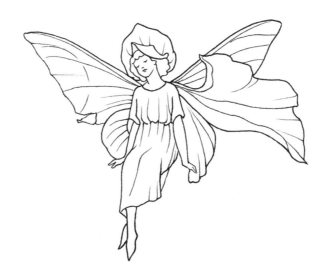

The FAIRIES A to Z Coloring Book

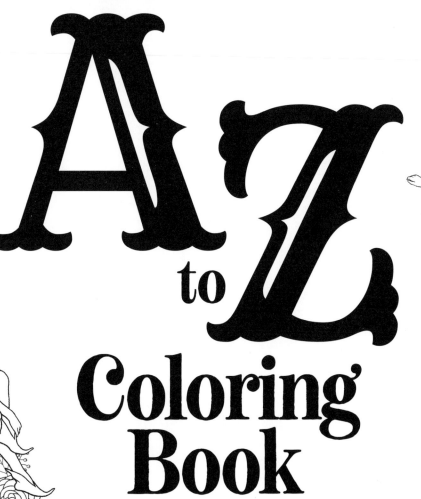

SIRIUS

SIRIUS

This edition published in 2024 by Sirius Publishing, a division of
Arcturus Publishing Limited,
26/27 Bickels Yard, 151–153 Bermondsey Street,
London SE1 3HA

ISBN: 978-1-3988-3635-8
CH011213NT
Supplier 29, Date 0224, PI 00005109

Printed in China

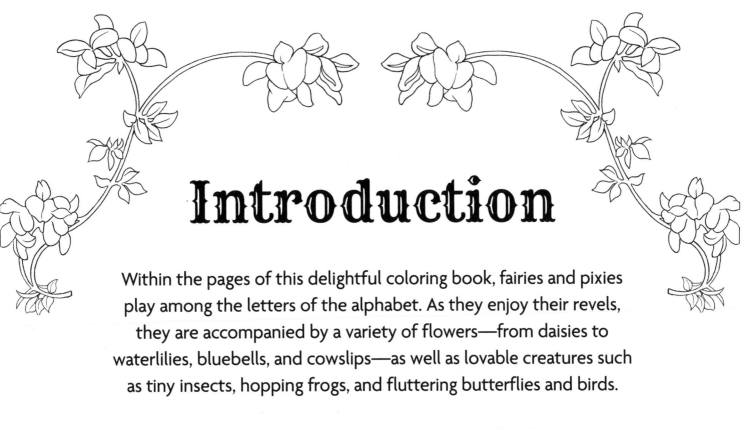

Introduction

Within the pages of this delightful coloring book, fairies and pixies play among the letters of the alphabet. As they enjoy their revels, they are accompanied by a variety of flowers—from daisies to waterlilies, bluebells, and cowslips—as well as lovable creatures such as tiny insects, hopping frogs, and fluttering butterflies and birds.

Evoking a sense of a simpler, bygone era, when the charm of fairy stories and pretty, colorful reading books helped small children to develop their imaginations and learn their letters, these images will transport you to a happy place.

Why not immerse yourself in this charming world: find yourself a quiet spot to settle down, select your coloring pens and pencils, and while away the hours as you bring these delicate illustrations to life.

Enjoy!

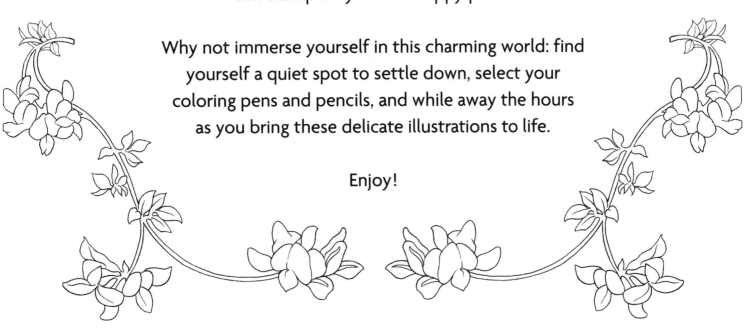

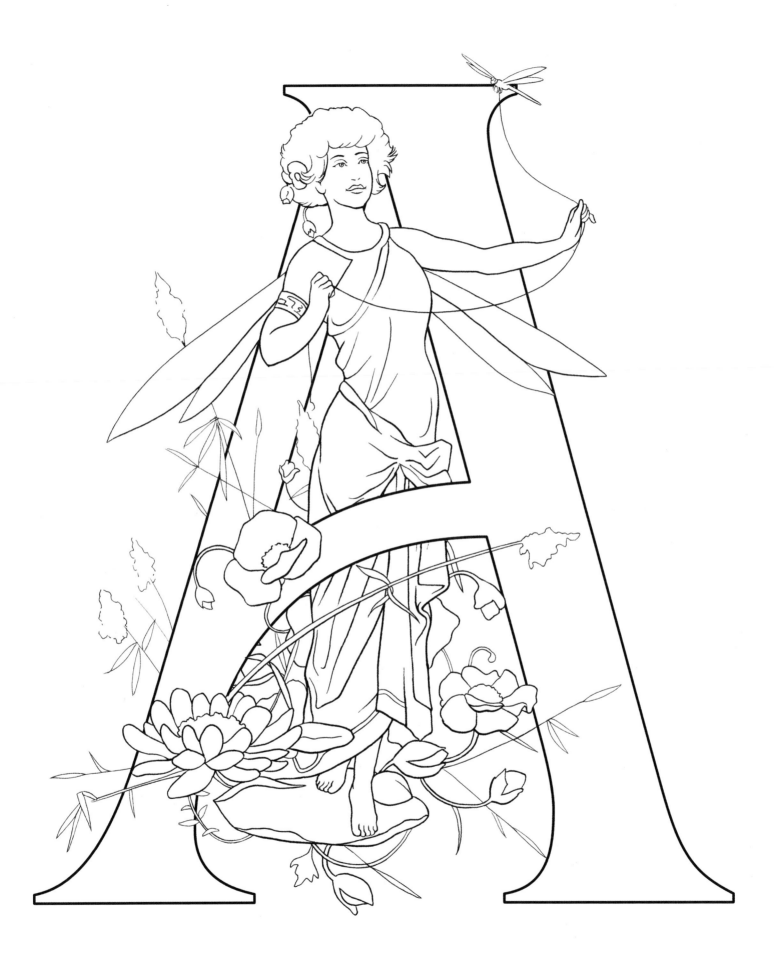

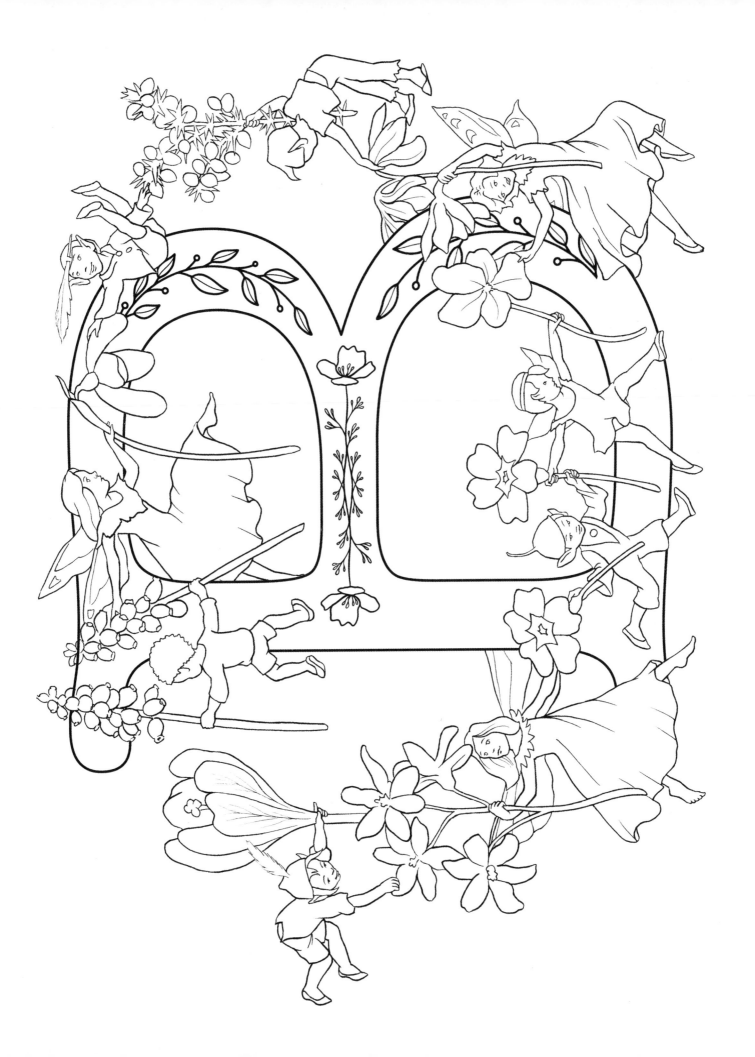

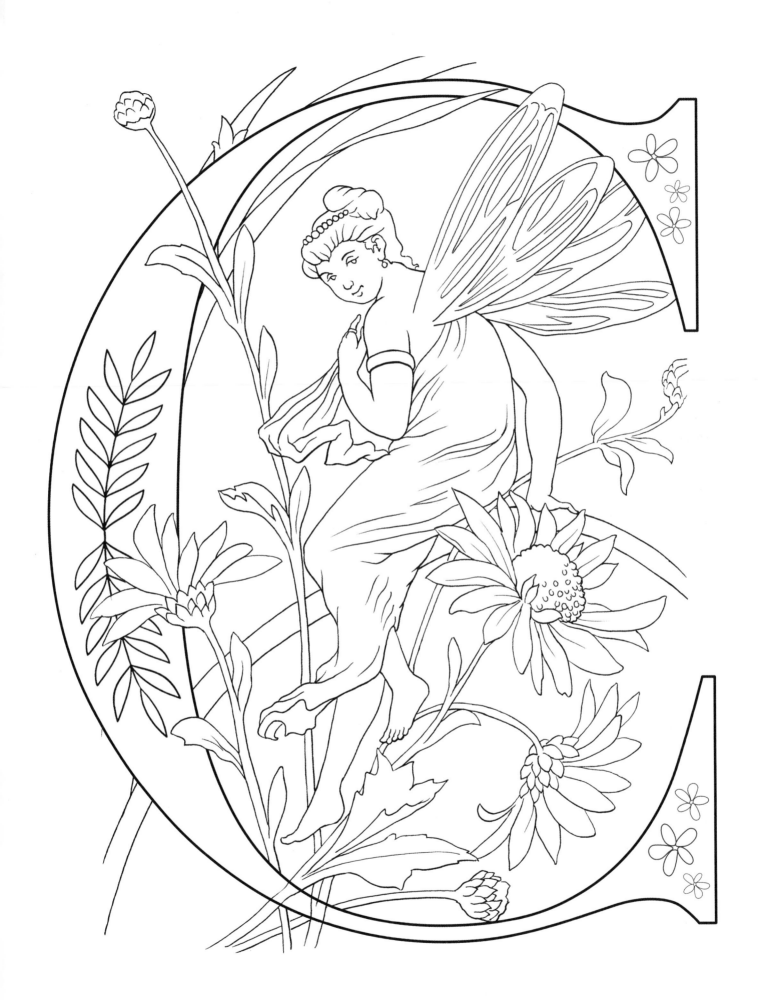

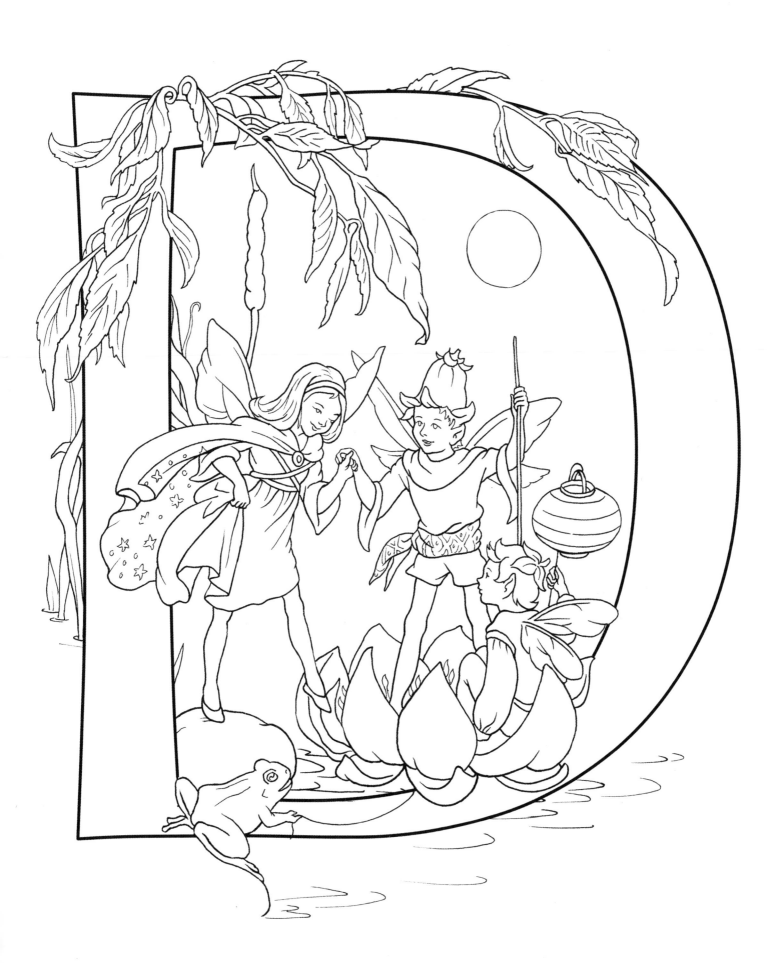

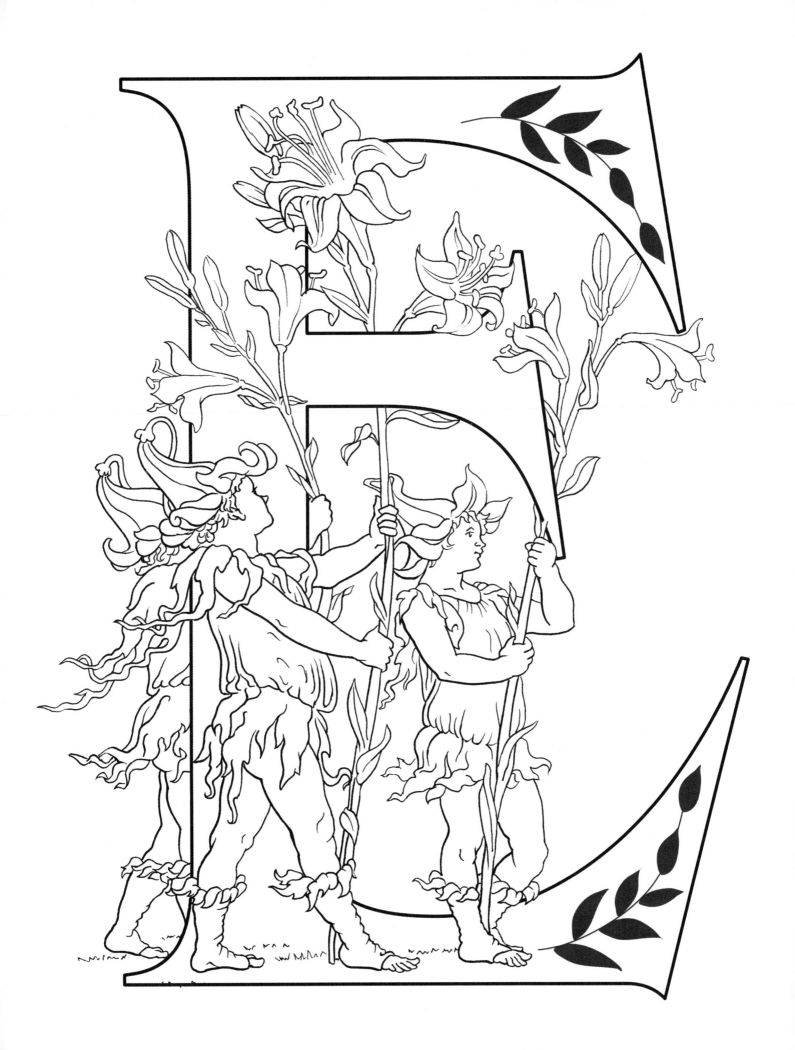

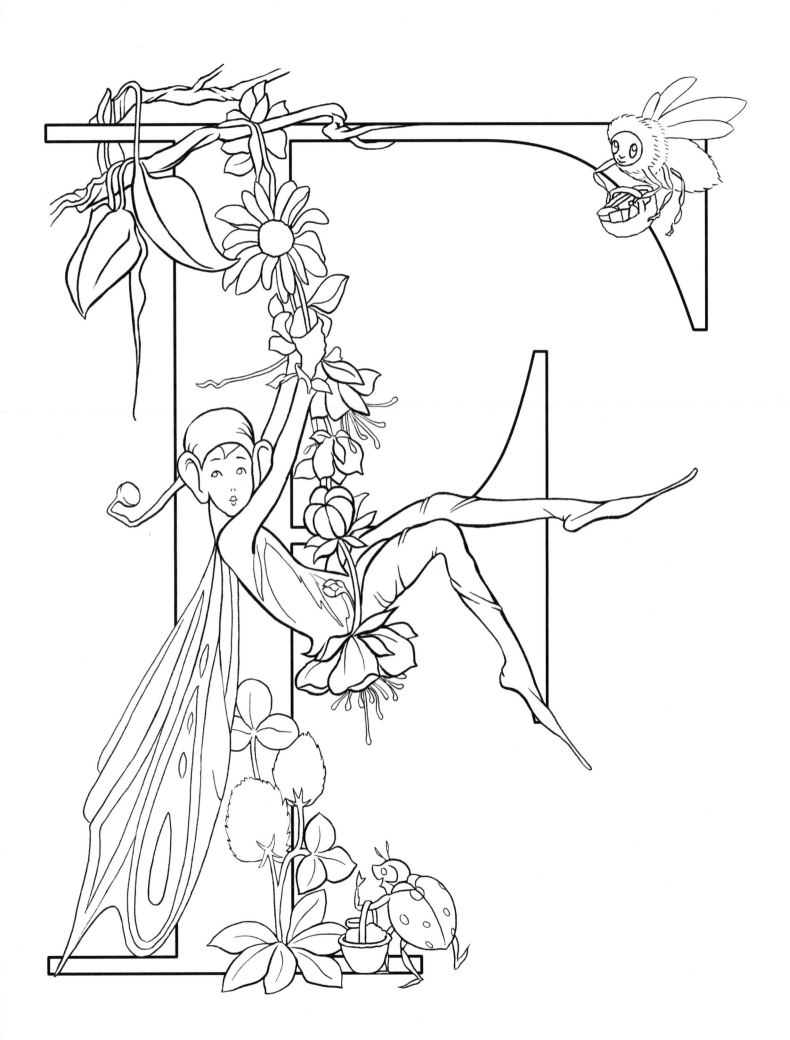

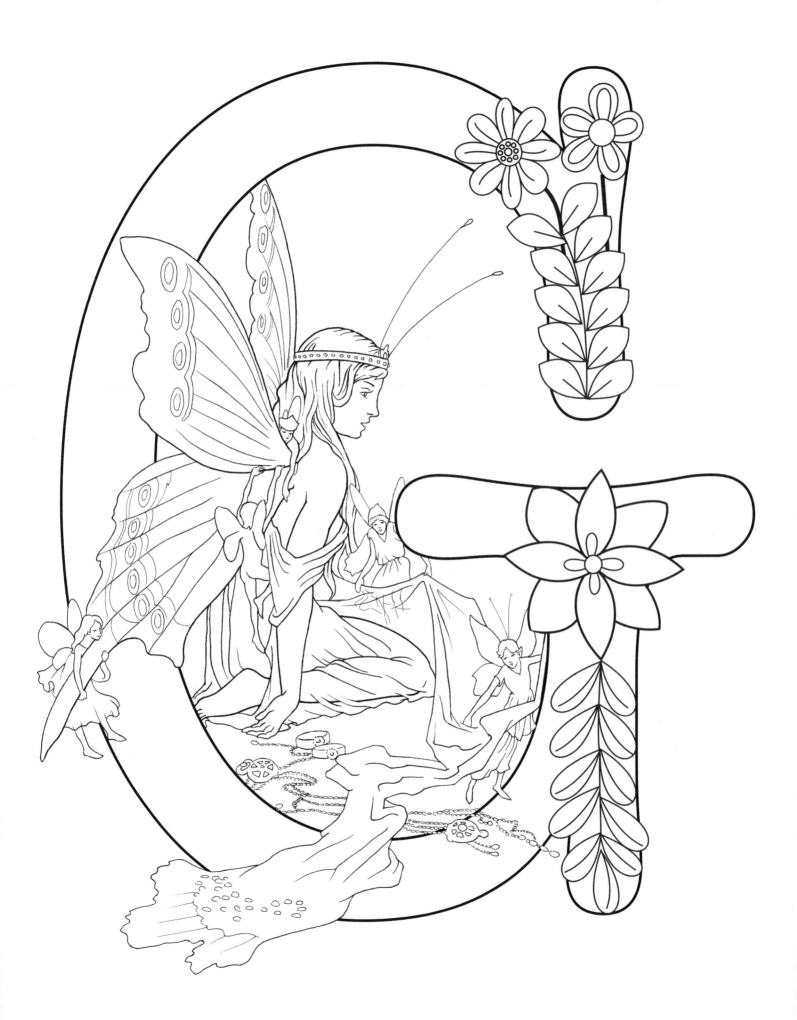

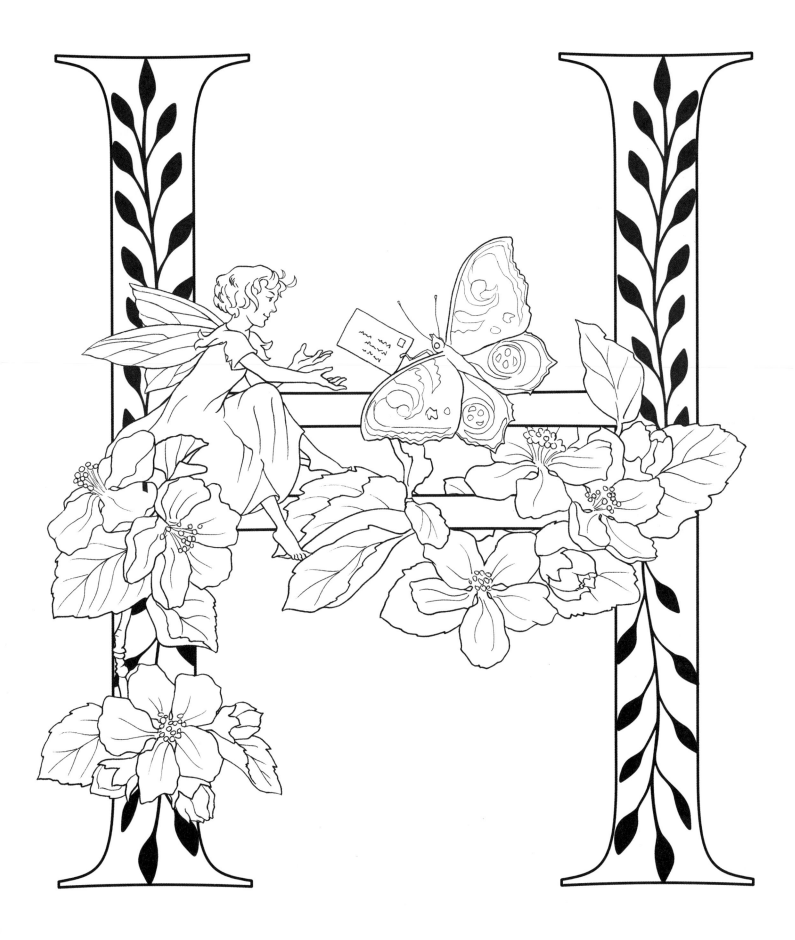

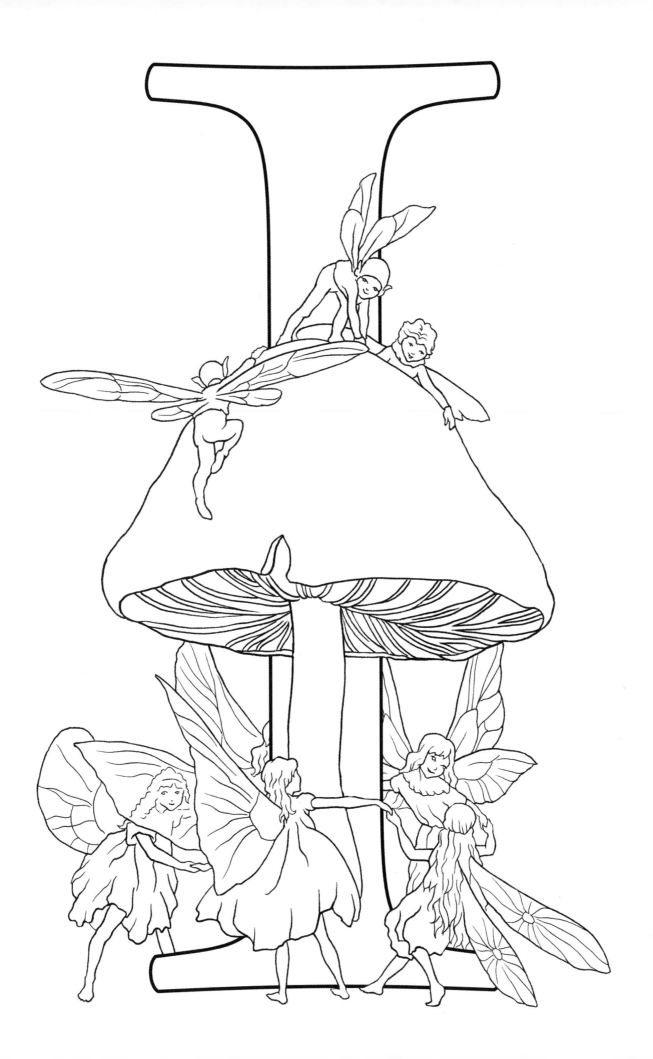

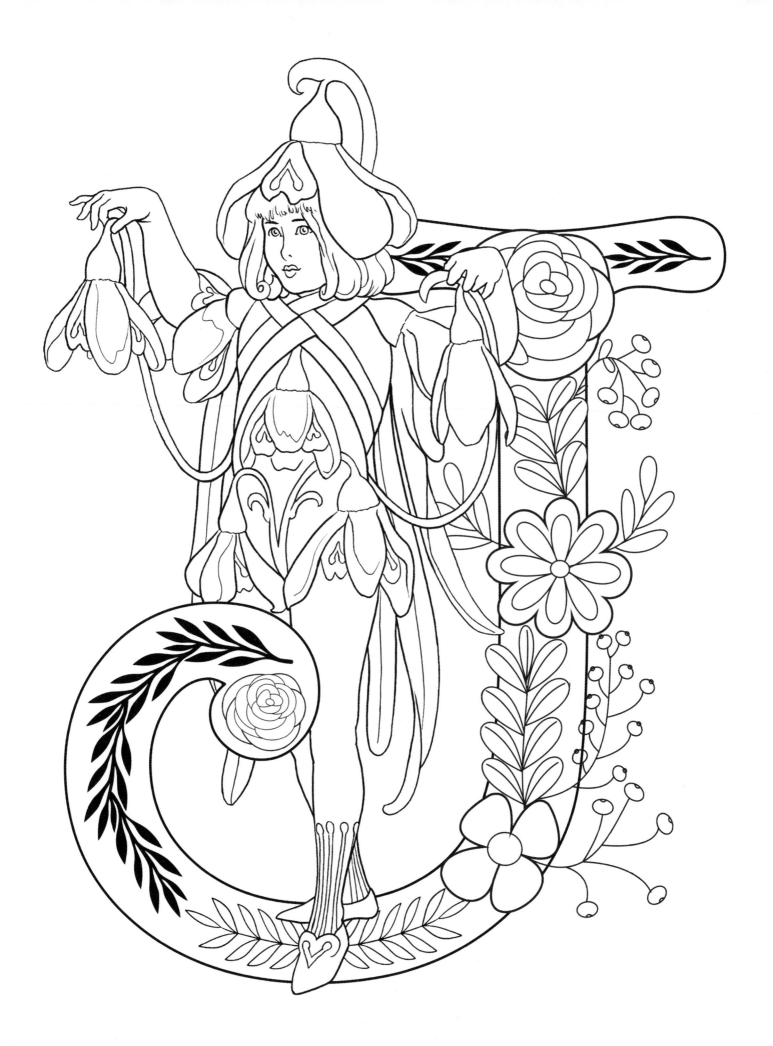

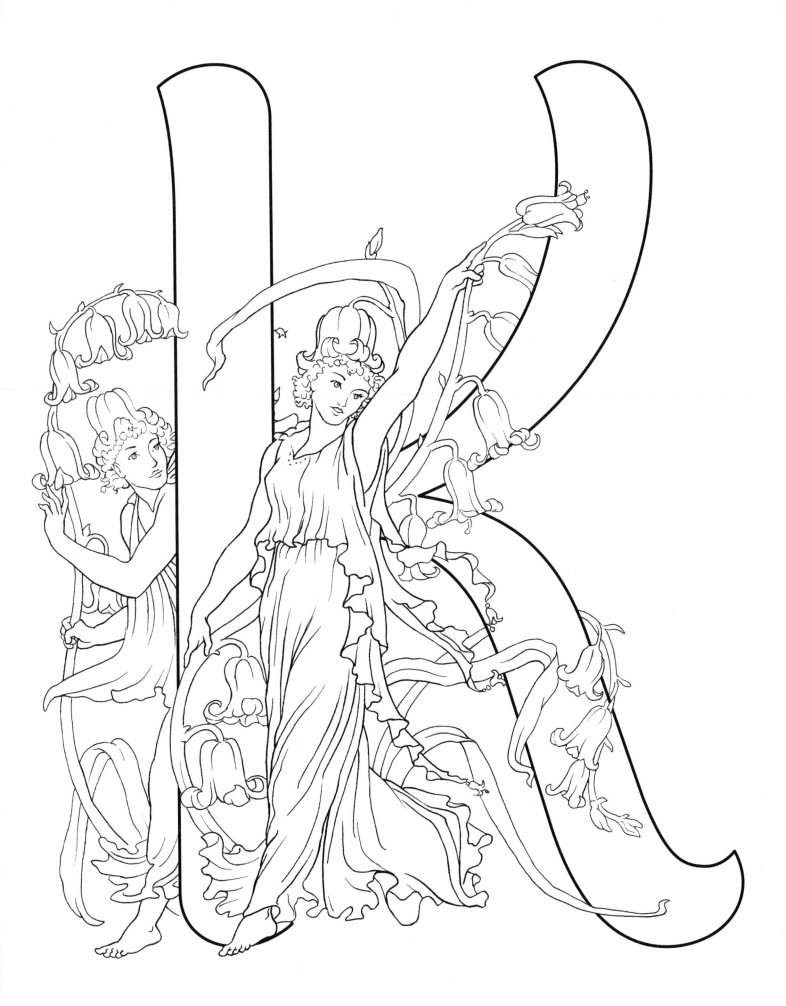

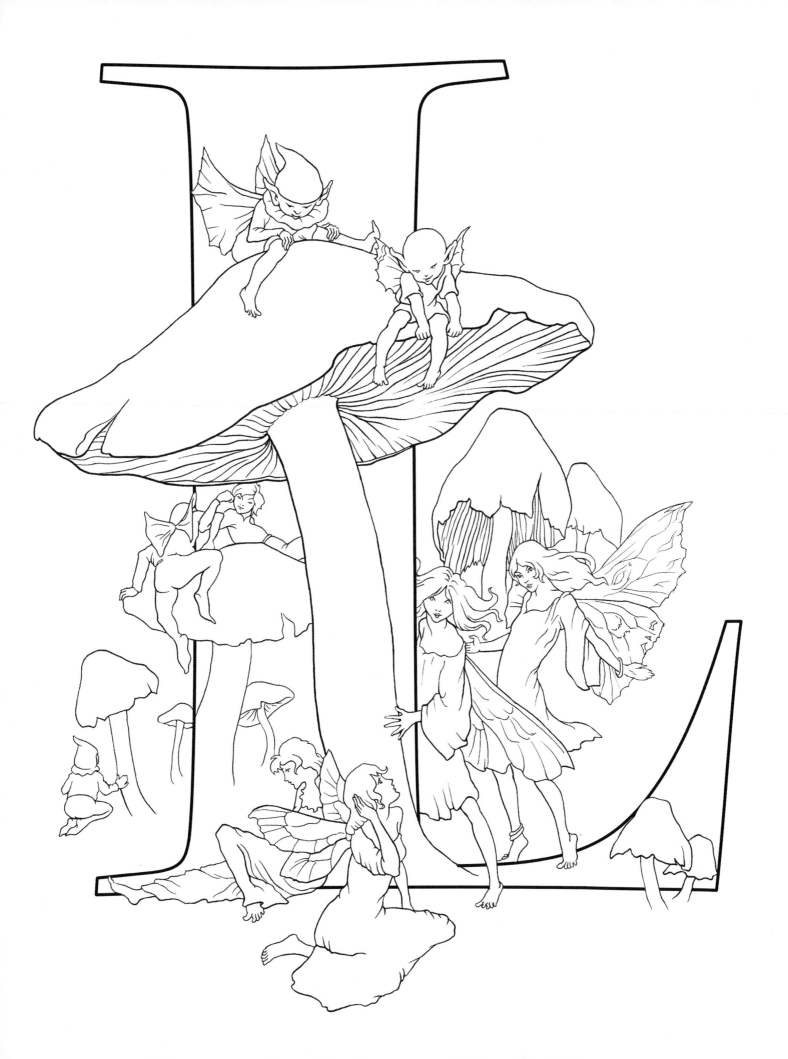

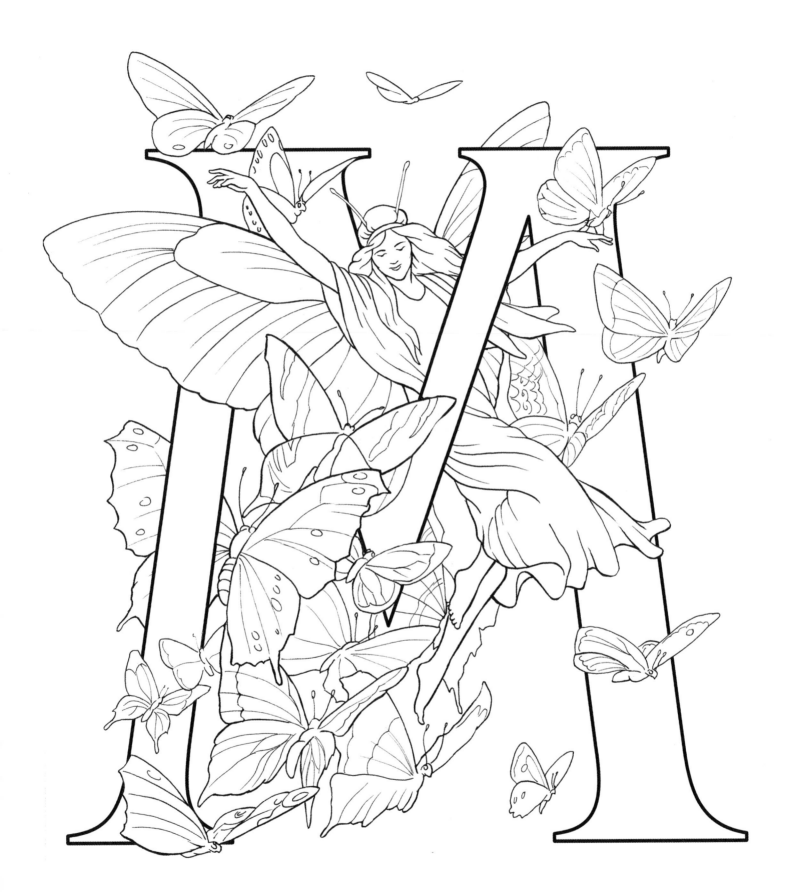

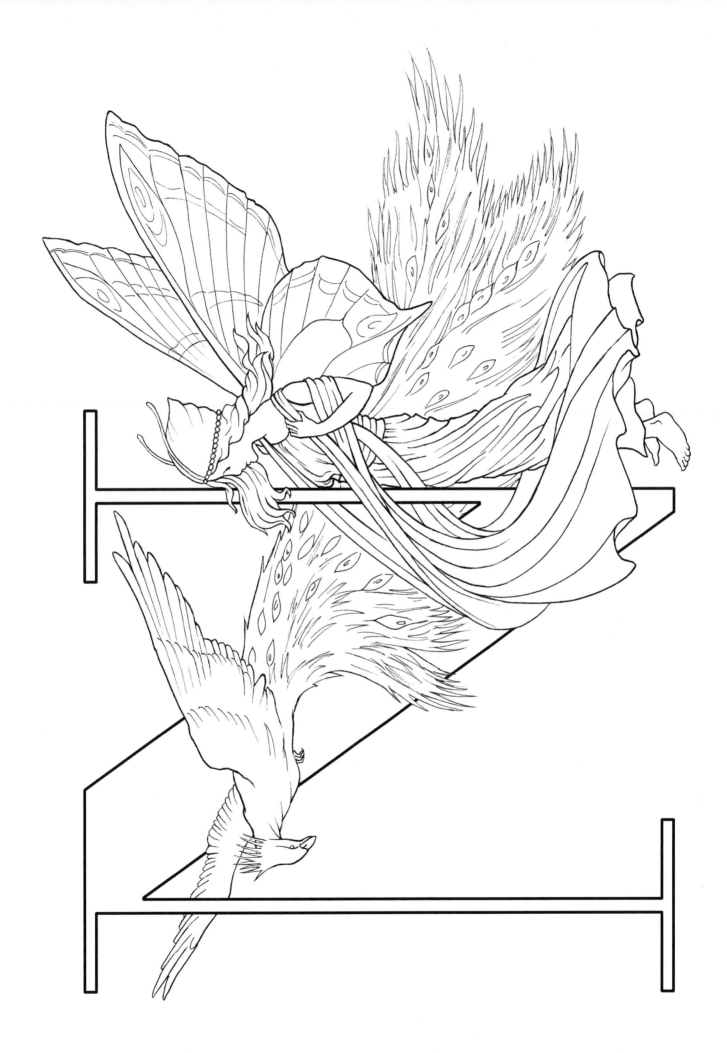

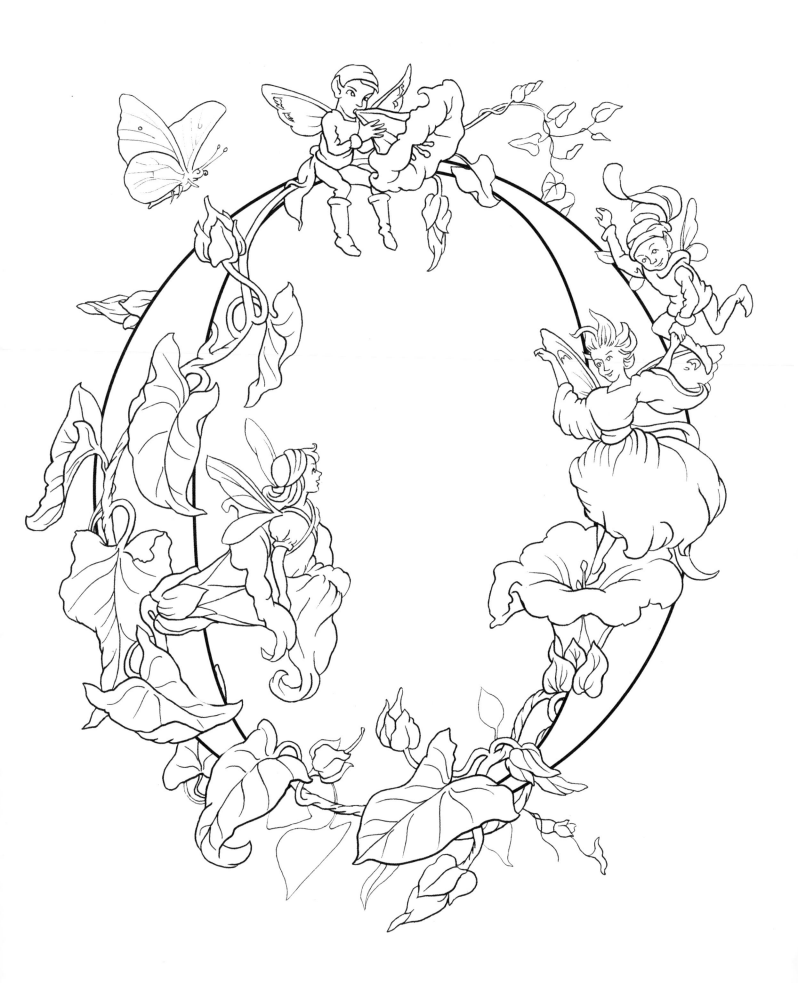

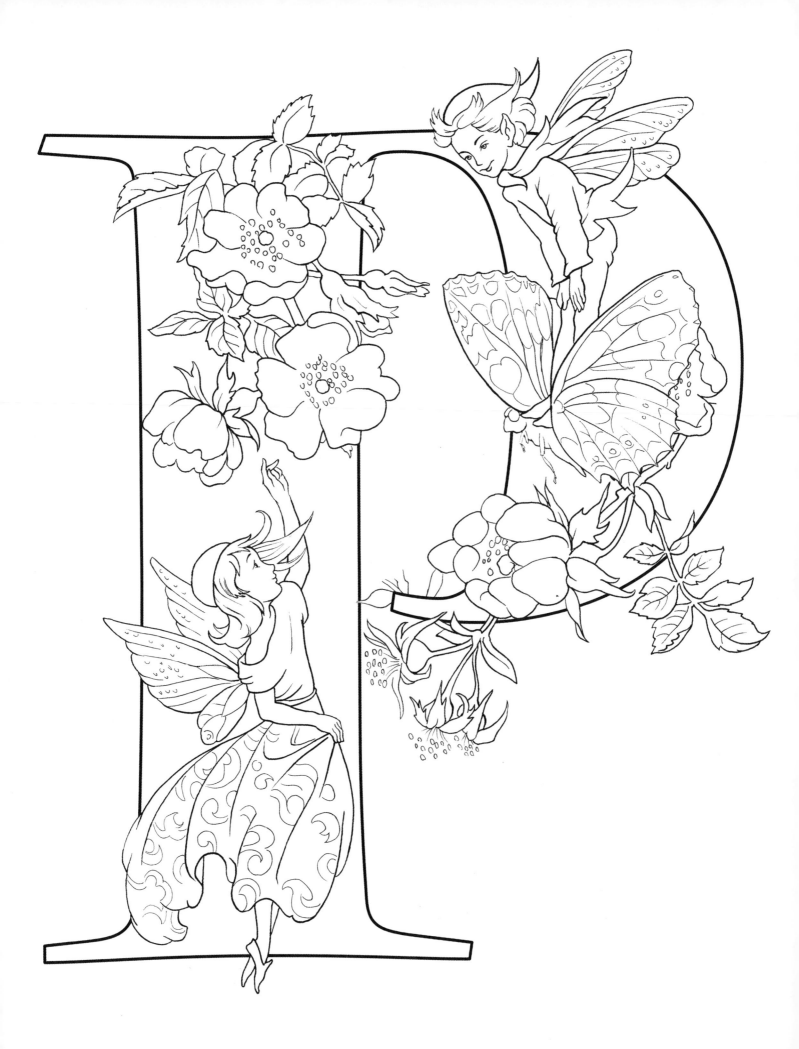

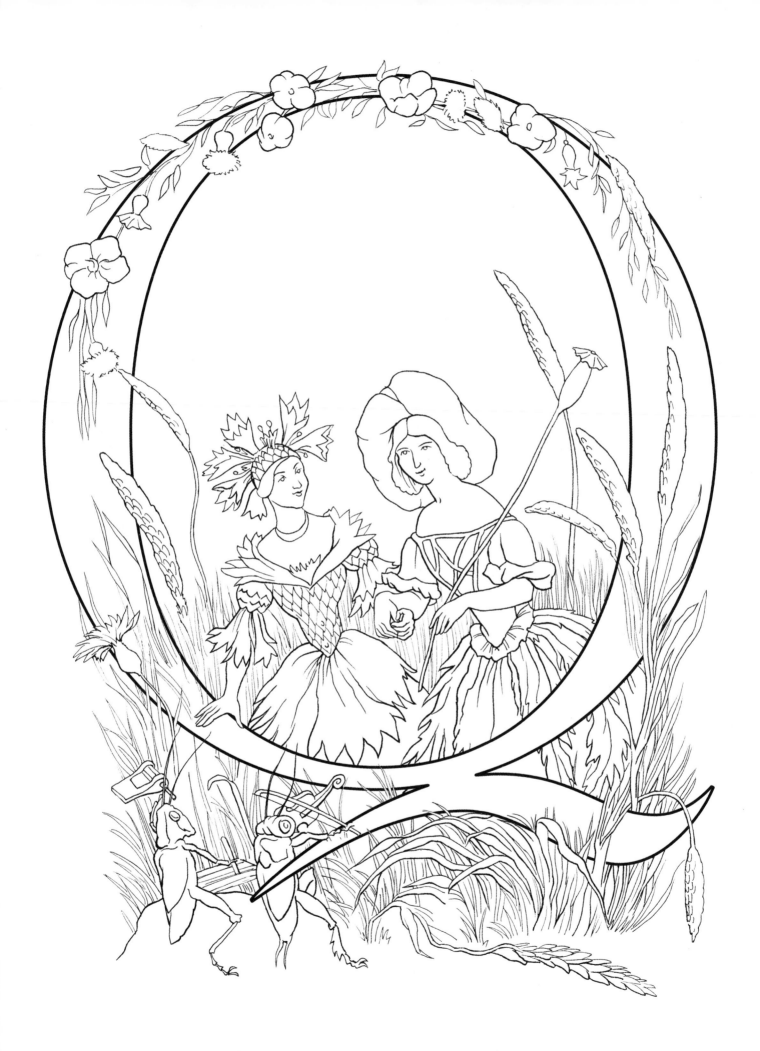

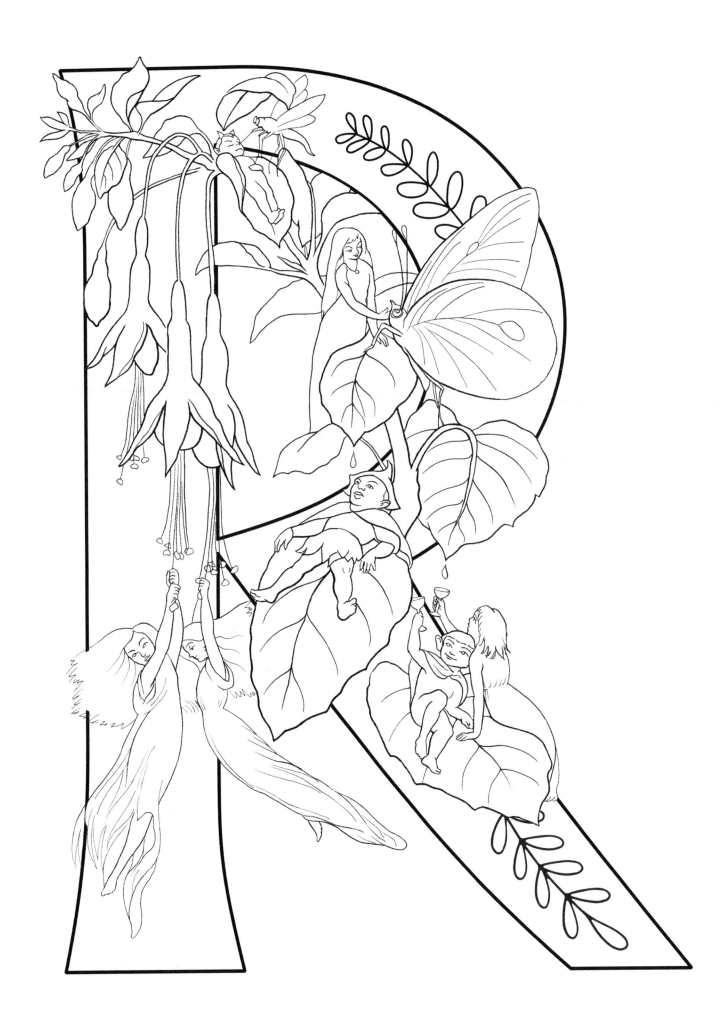

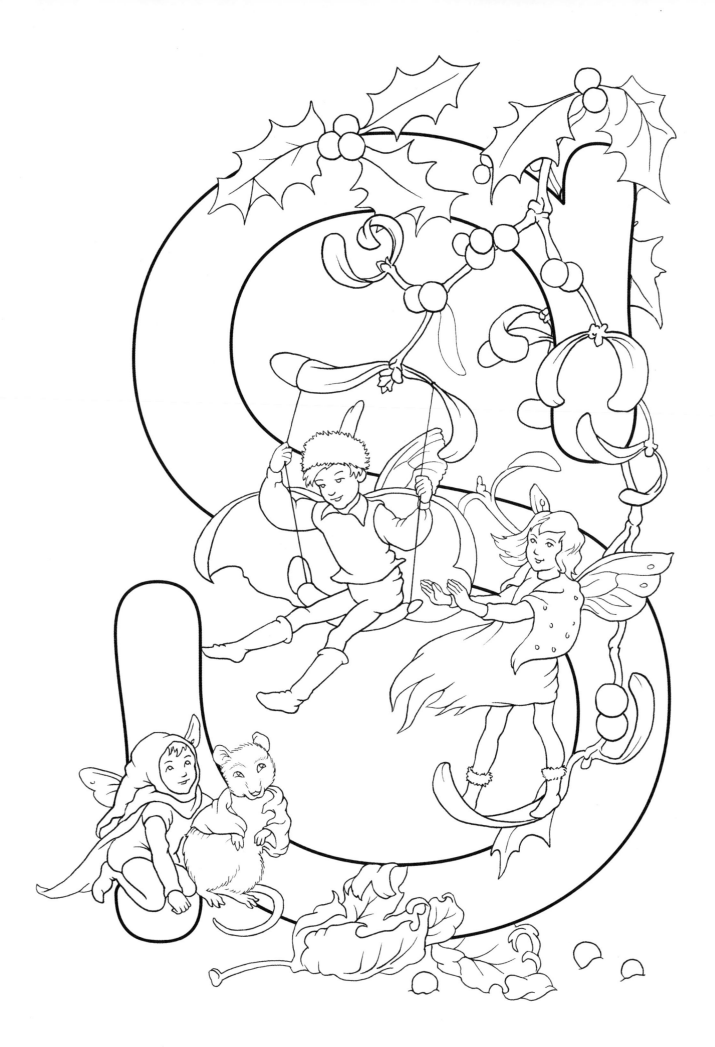

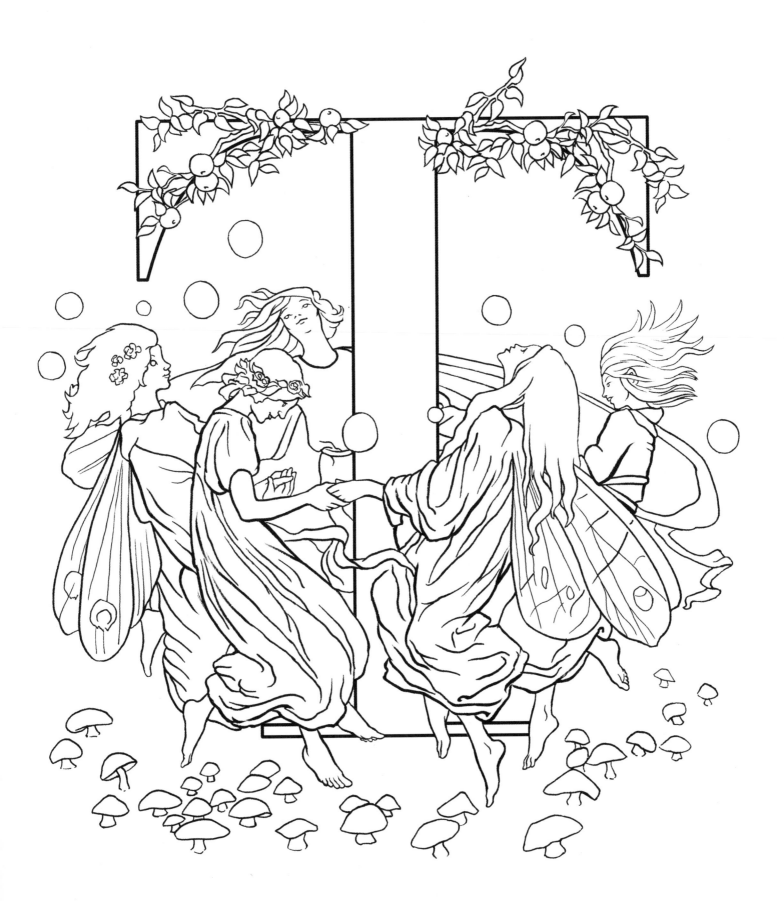

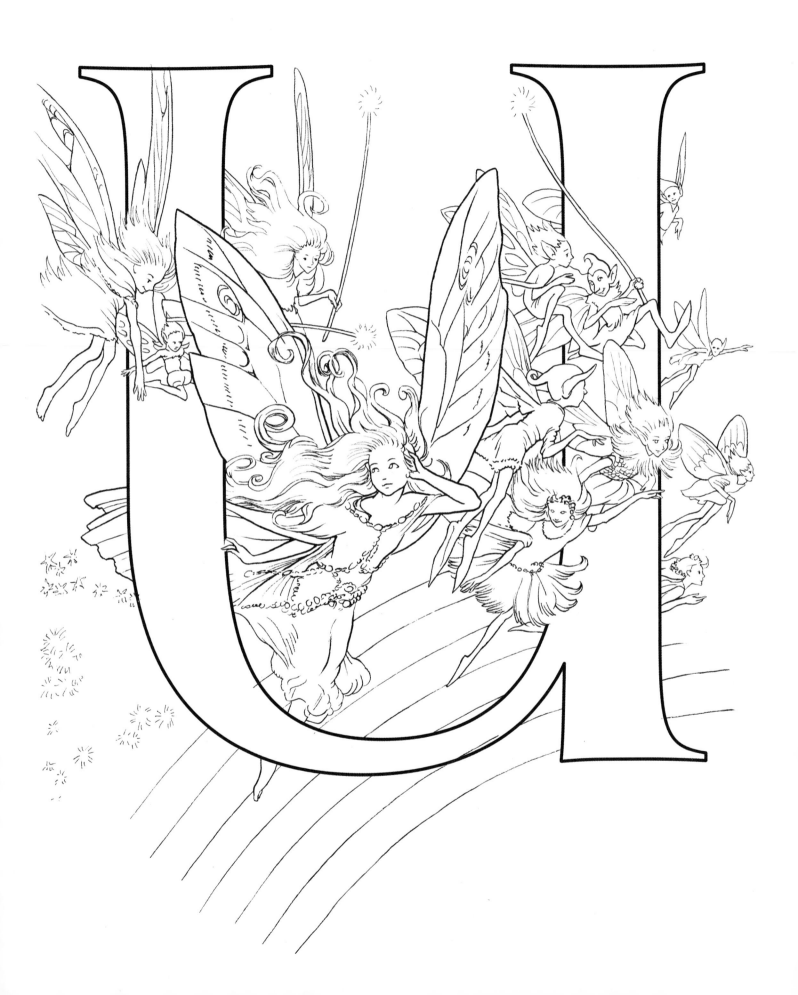

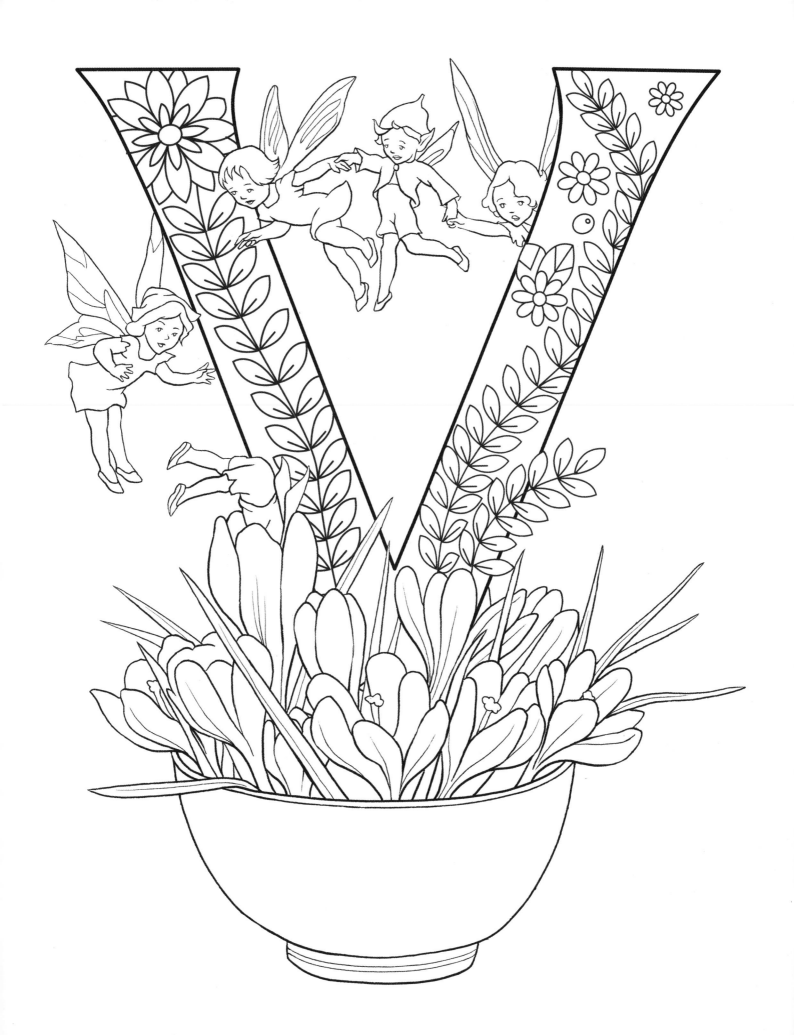

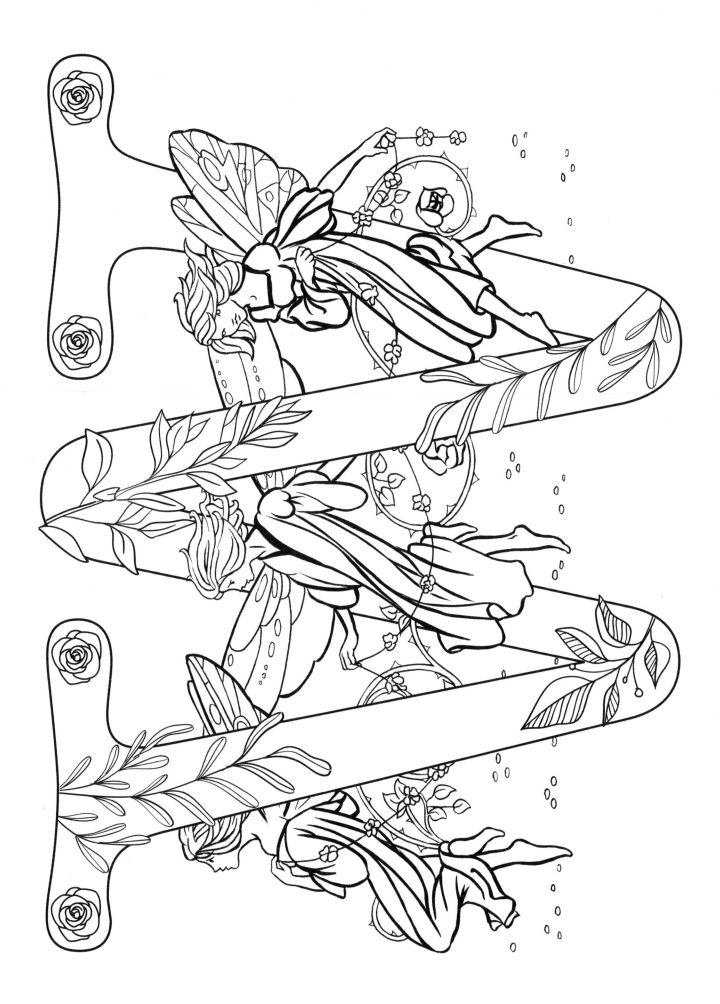

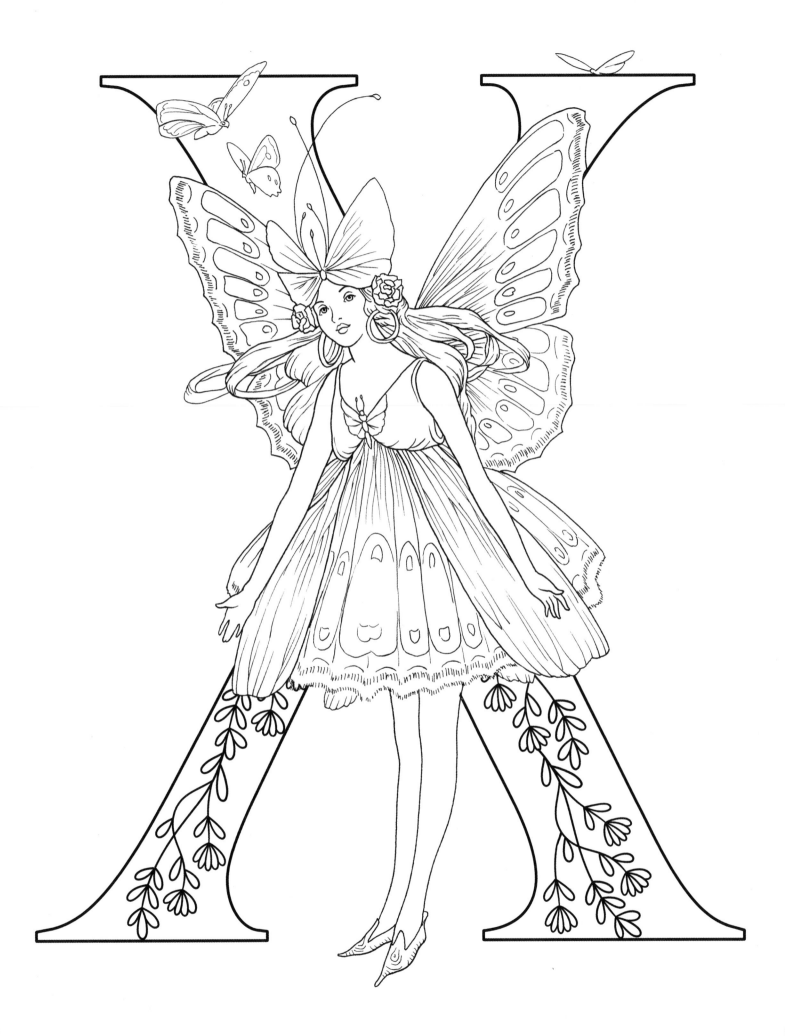

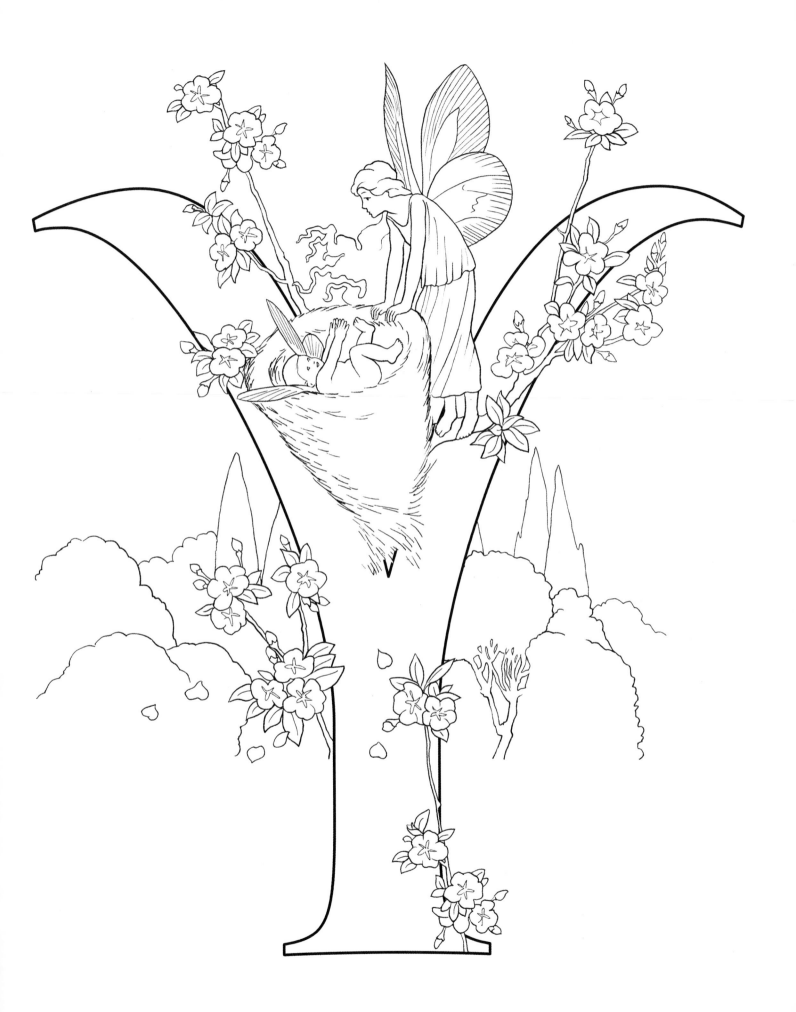

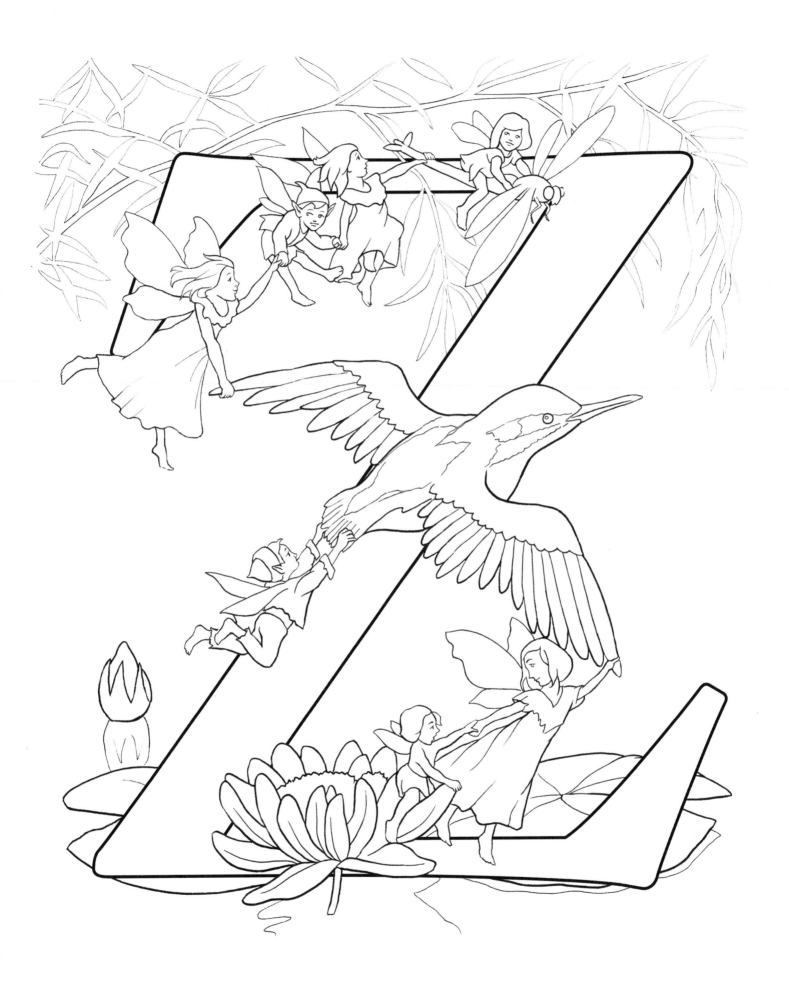

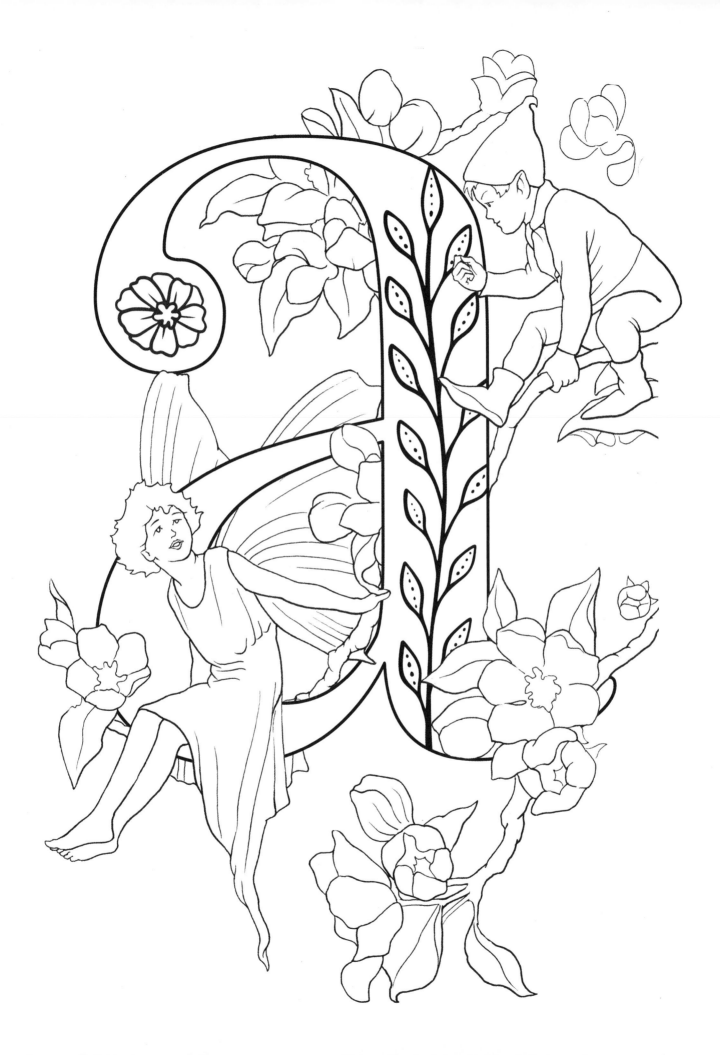

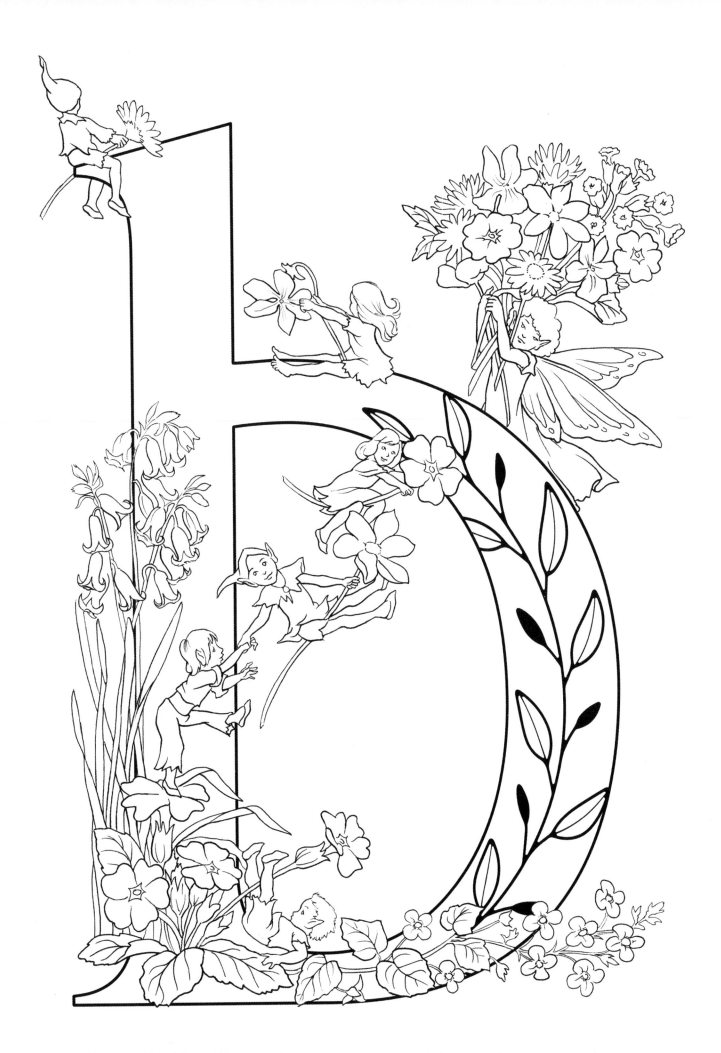

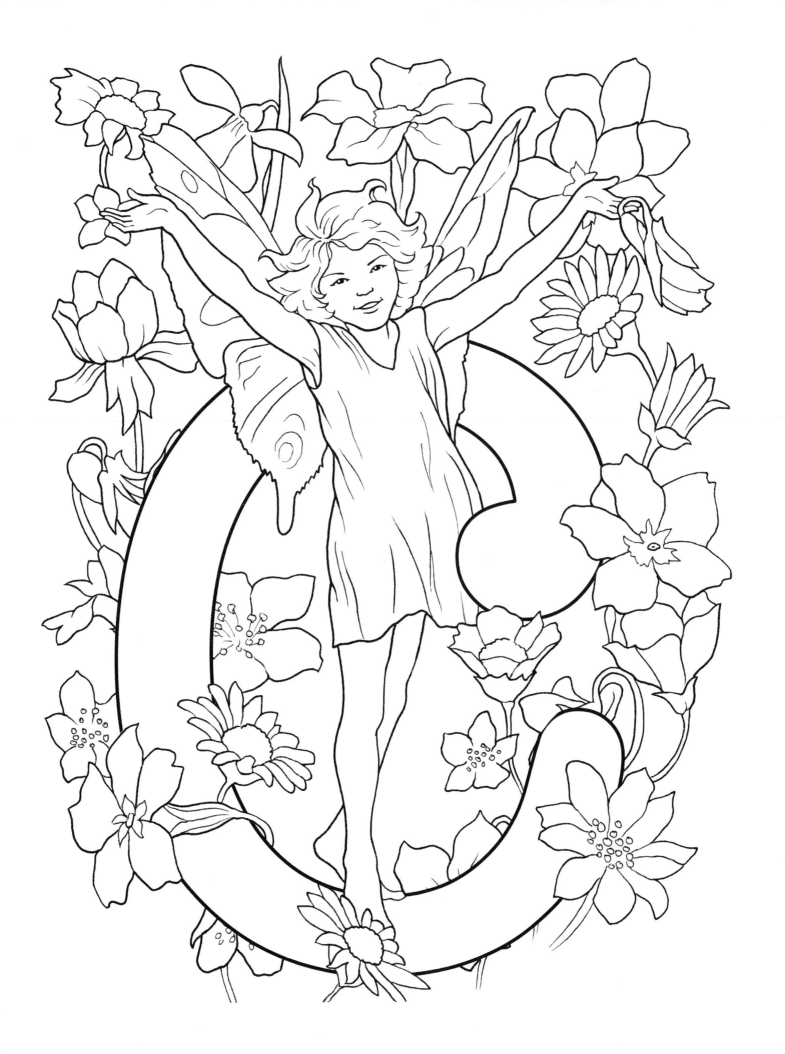

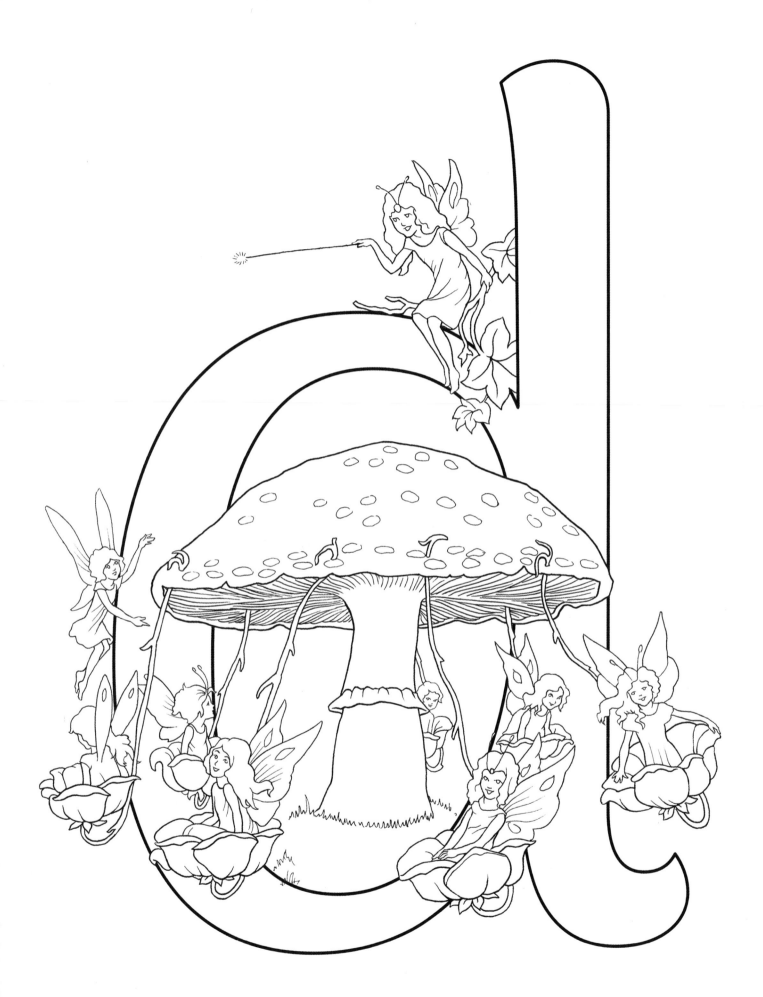

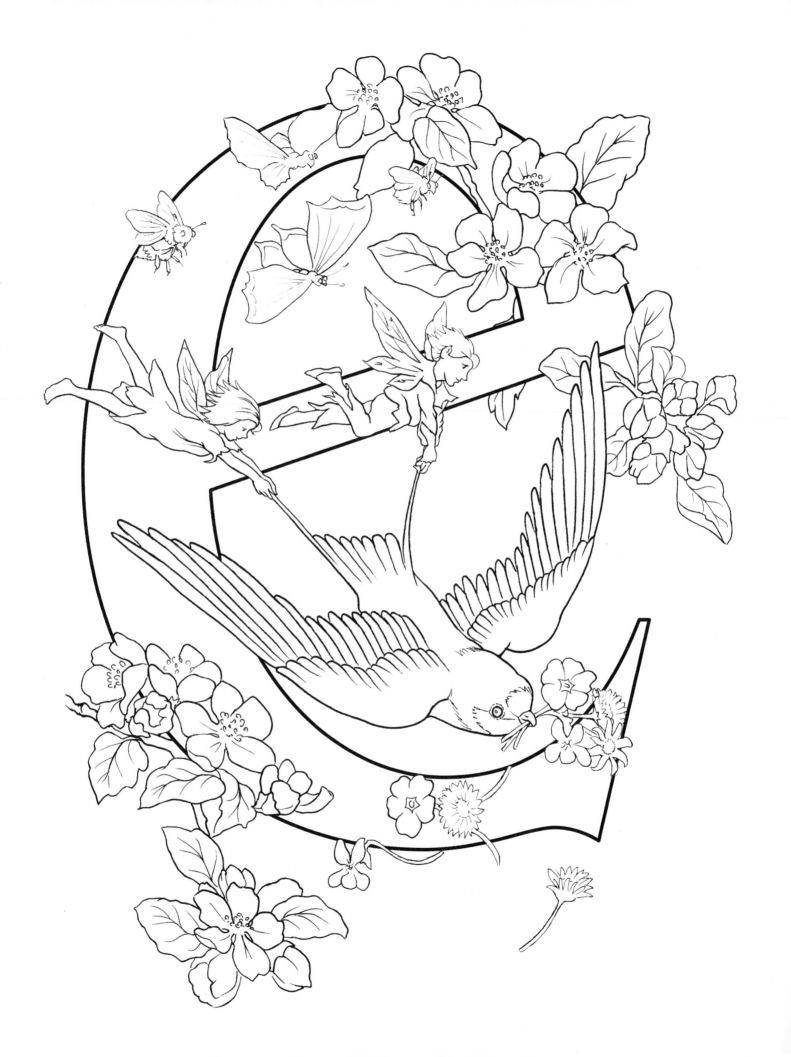

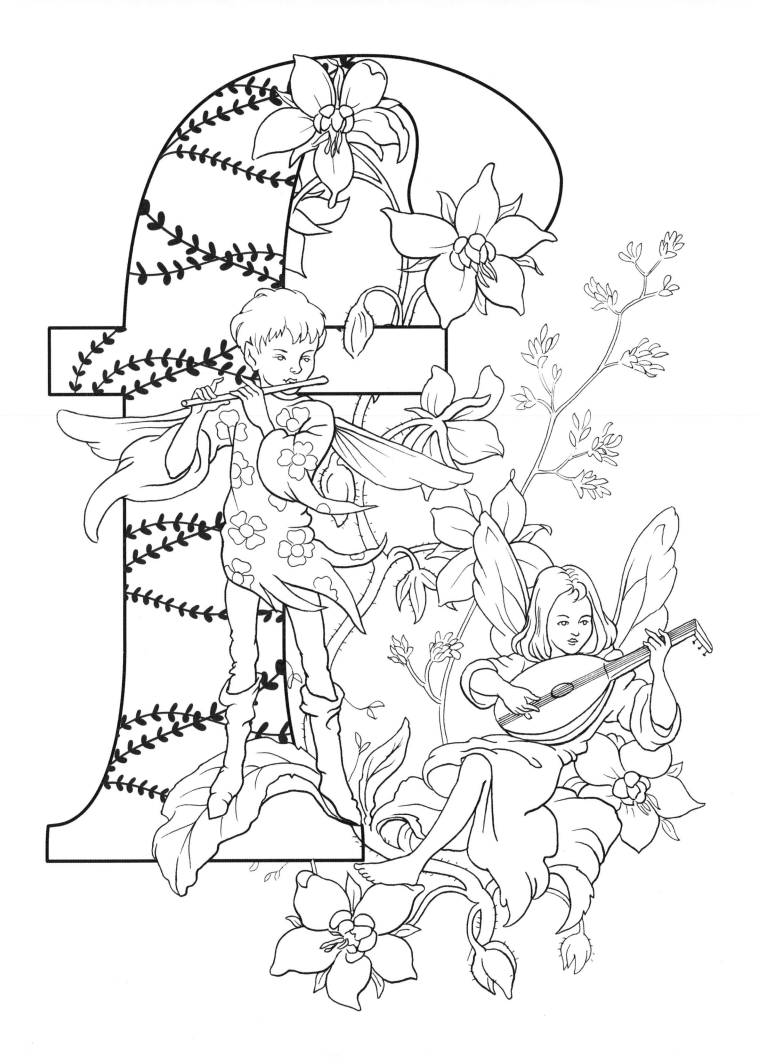

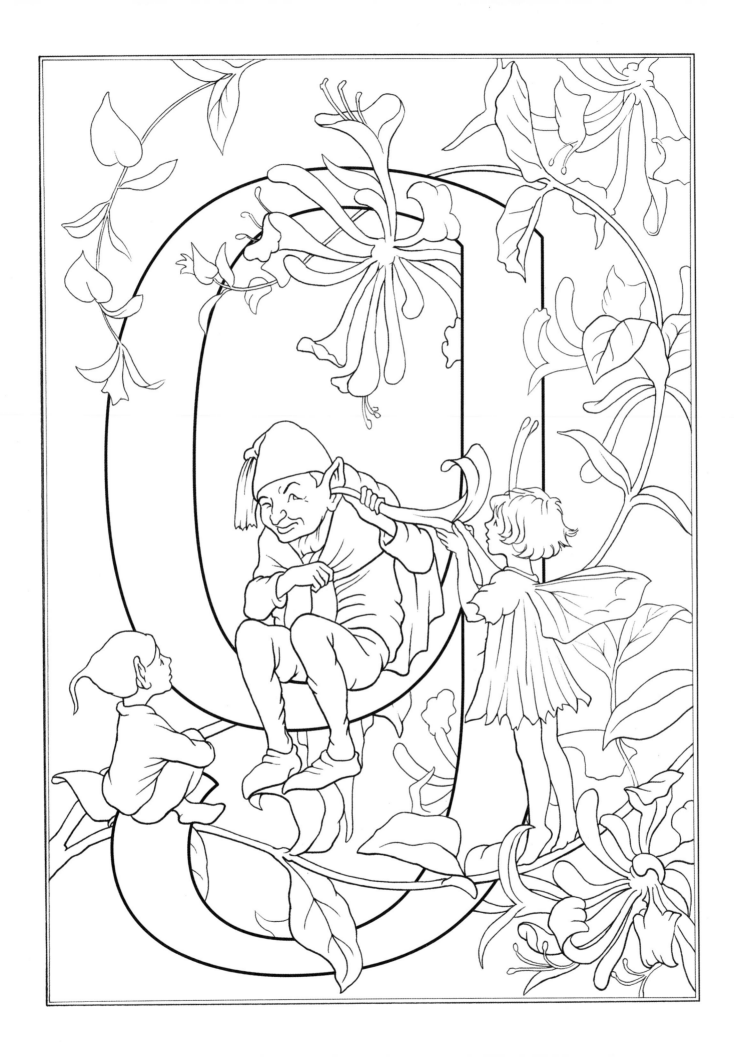

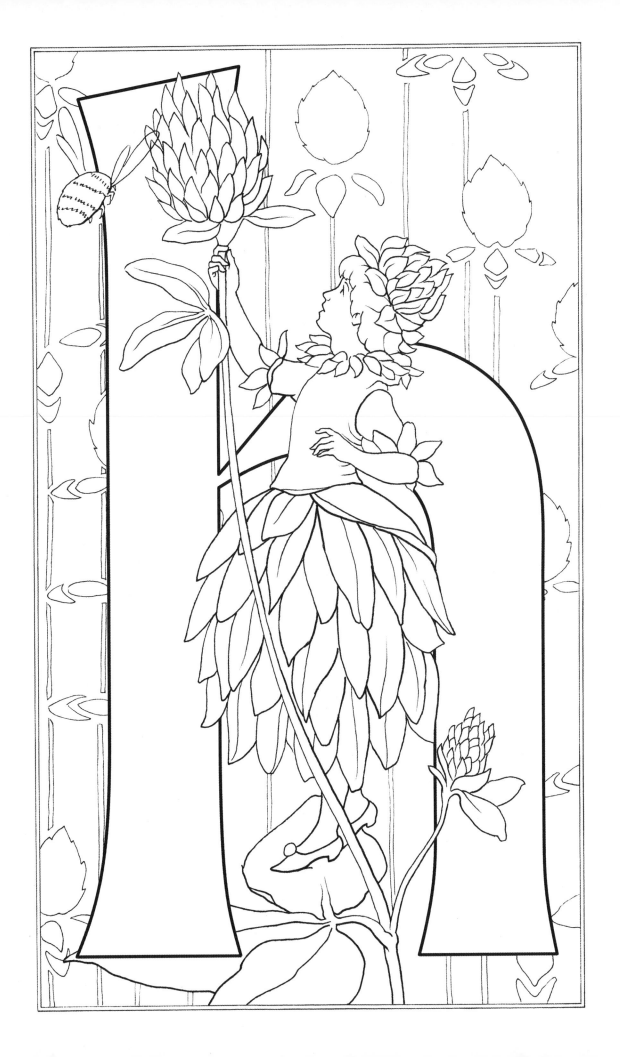

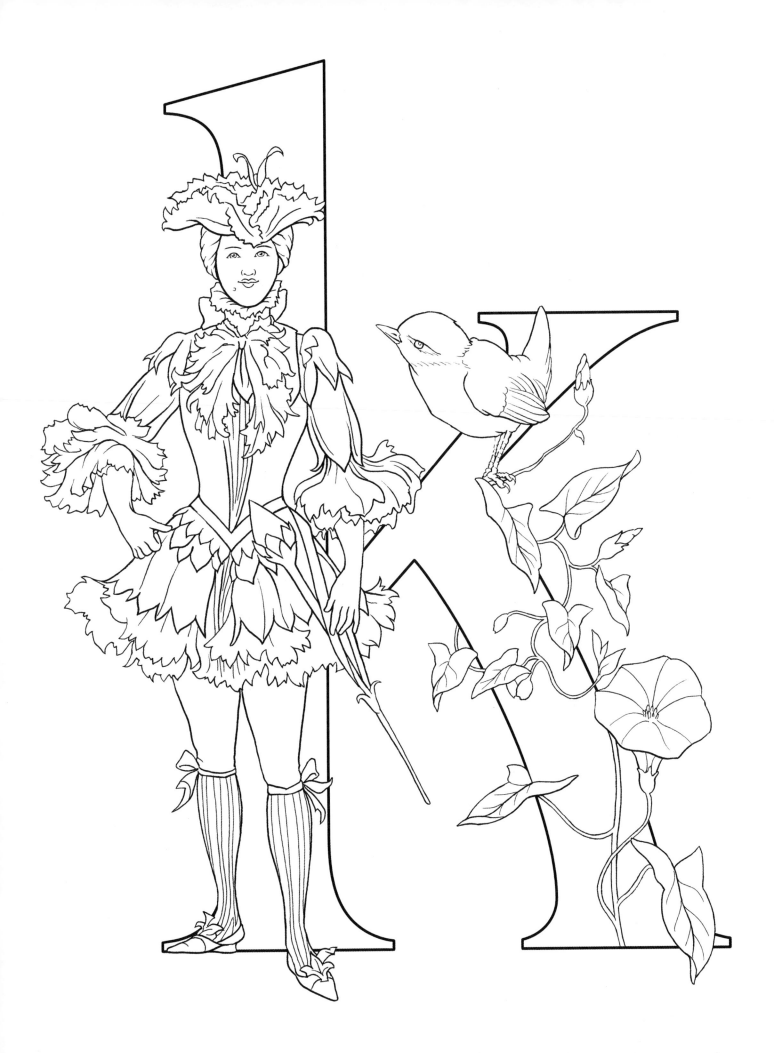

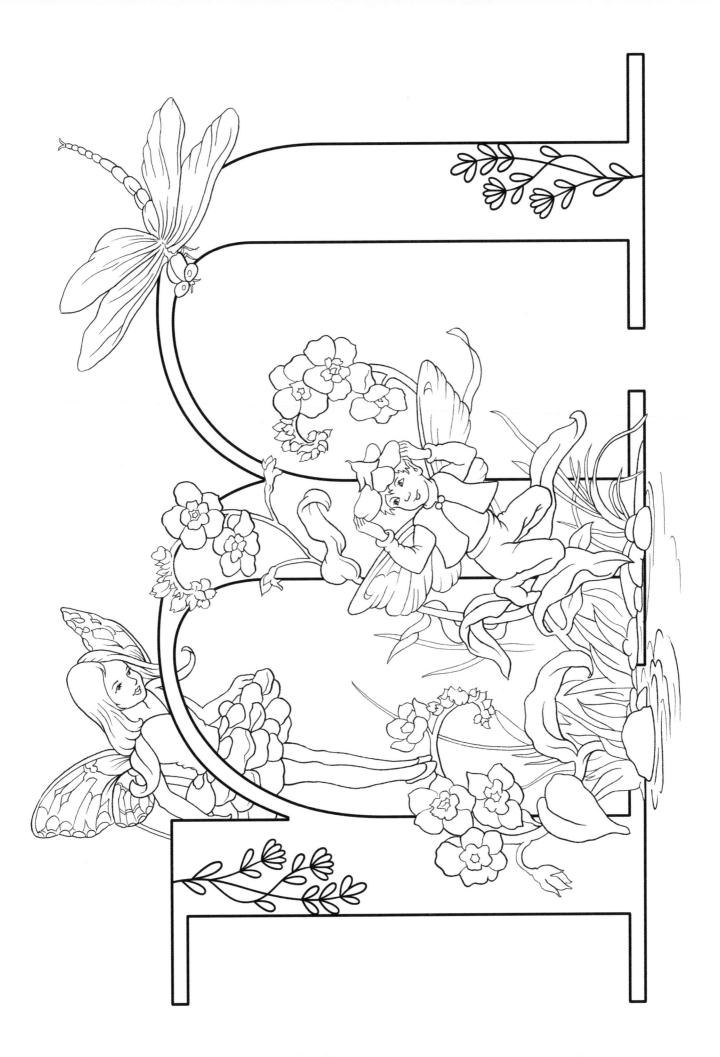

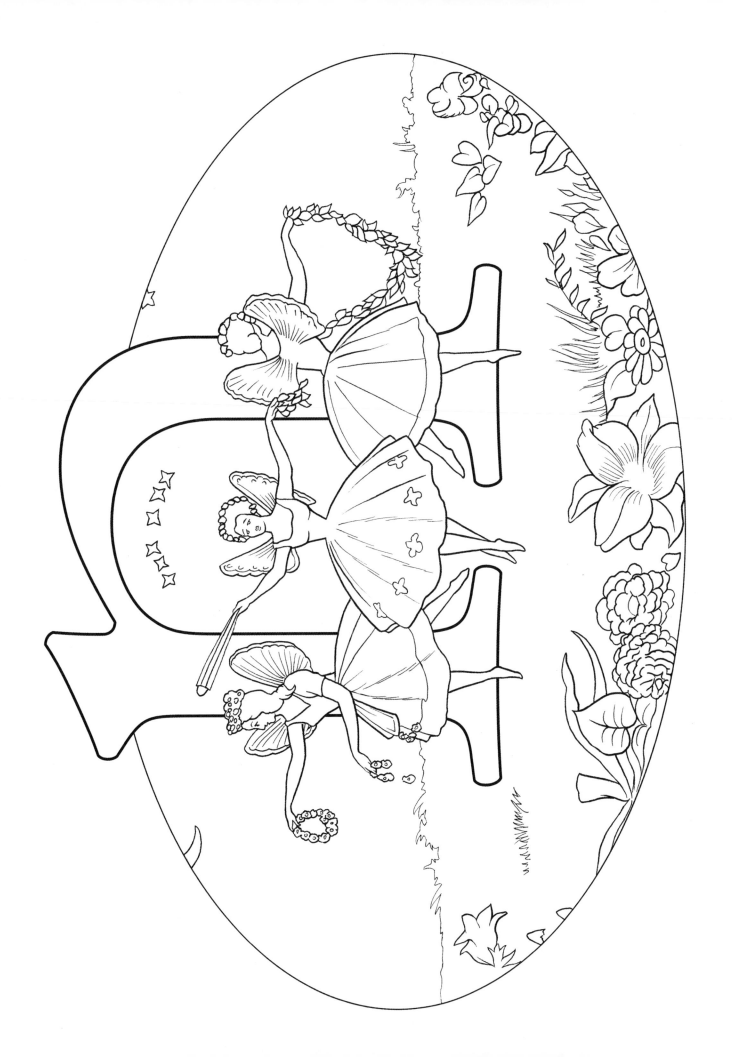

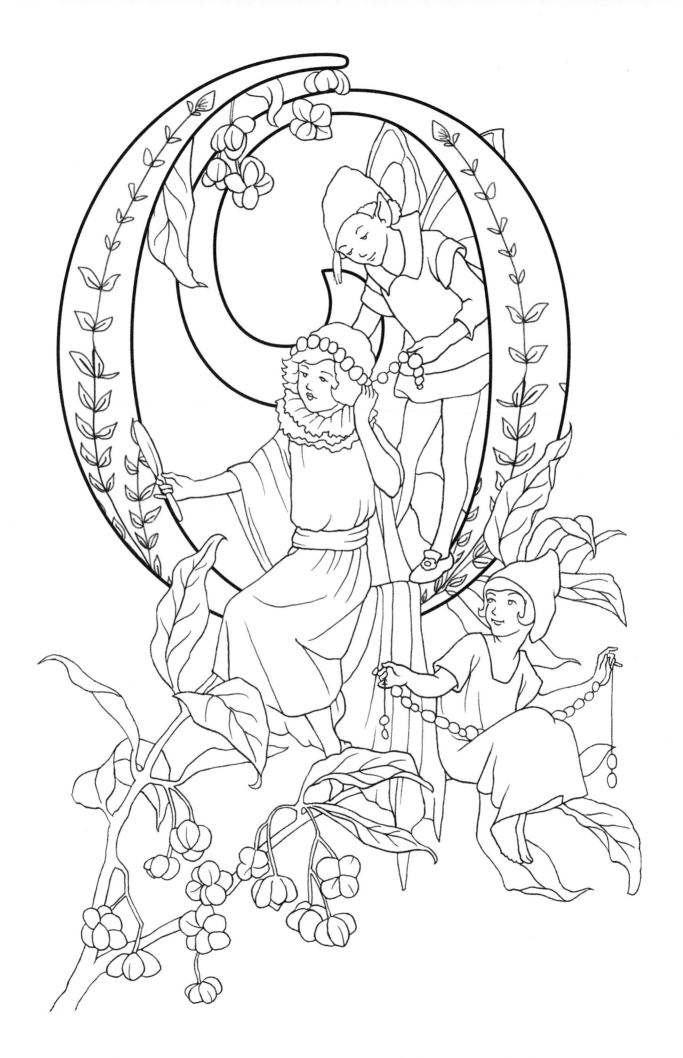

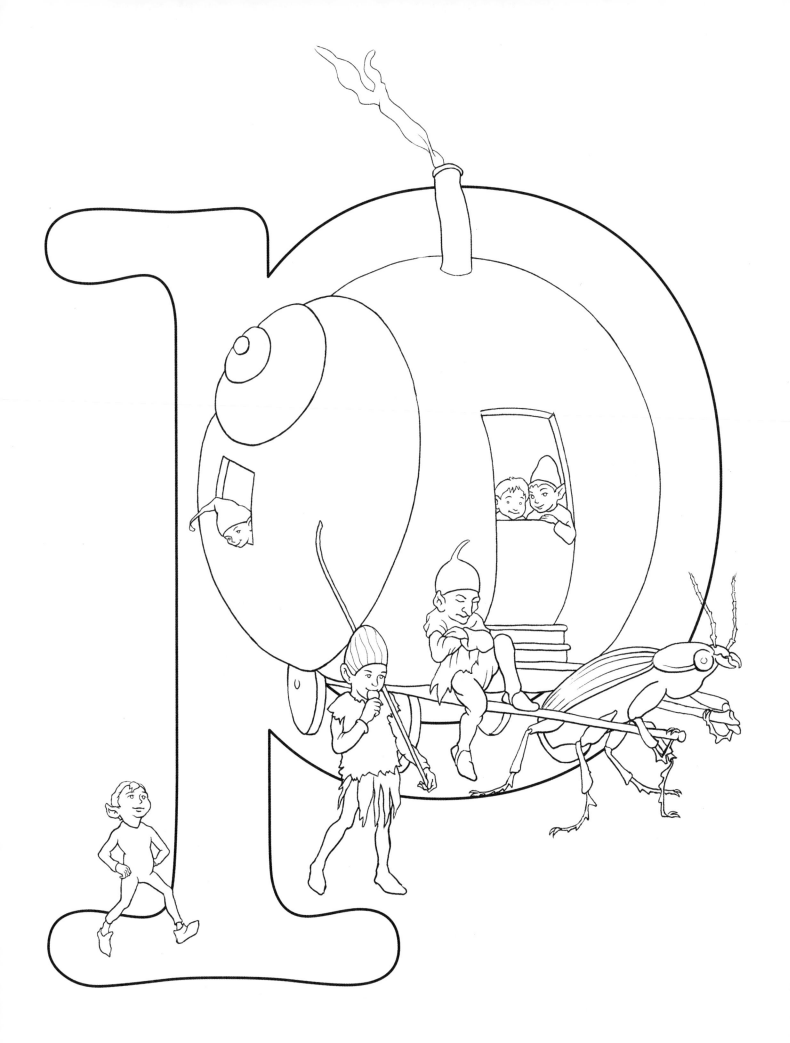

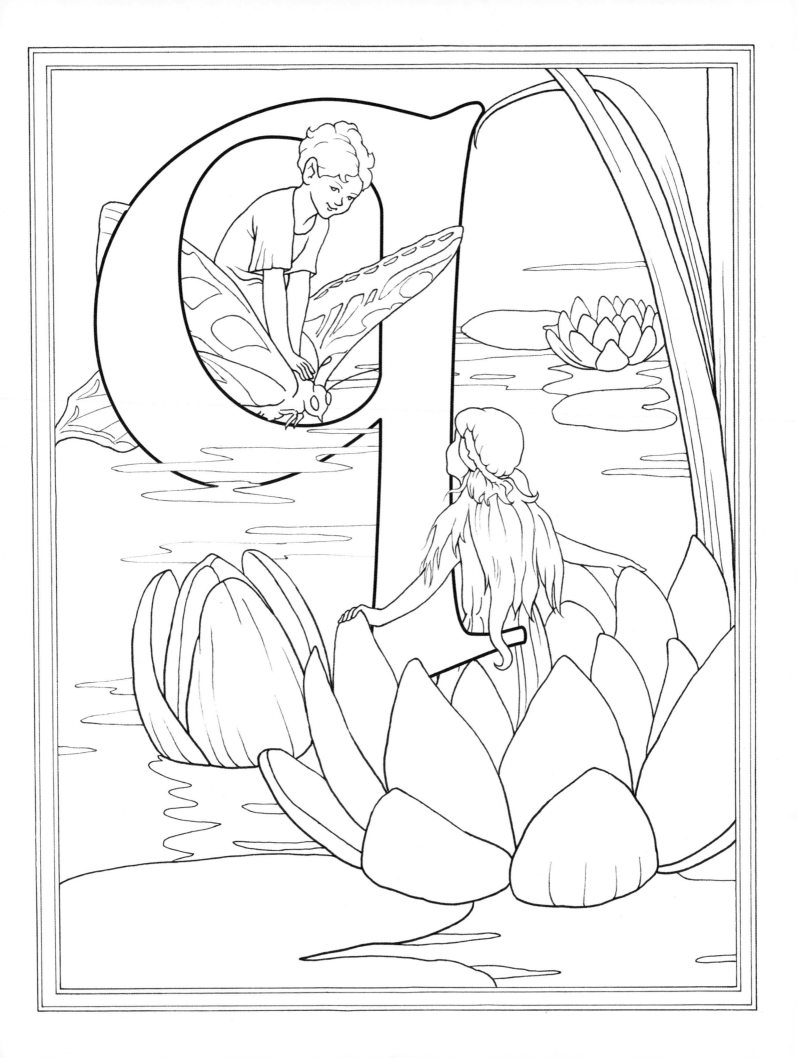

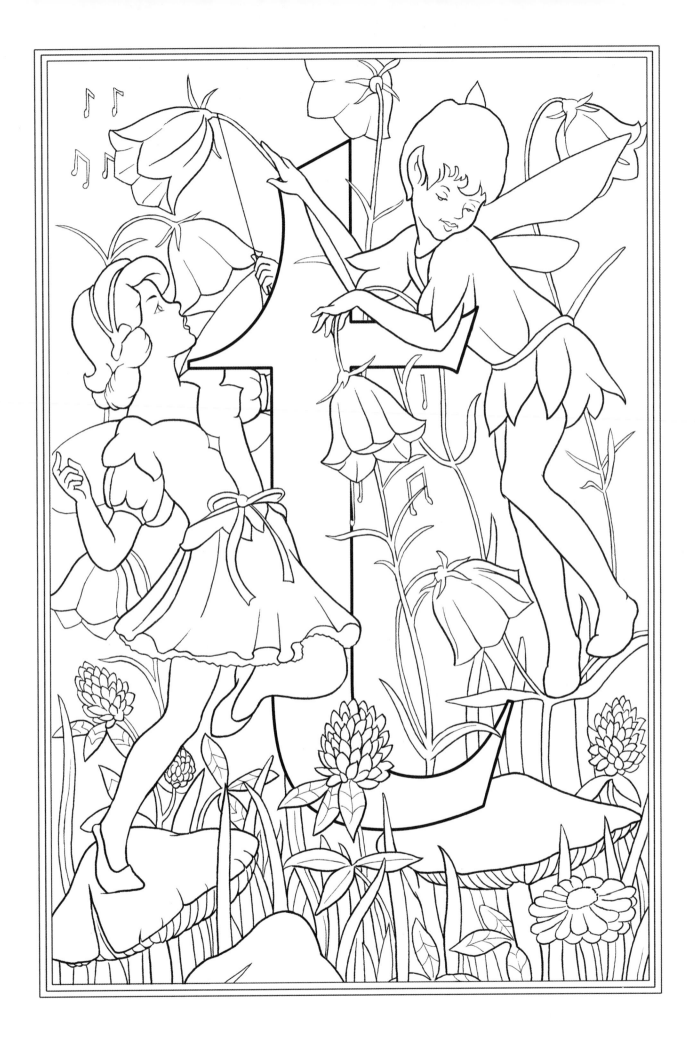

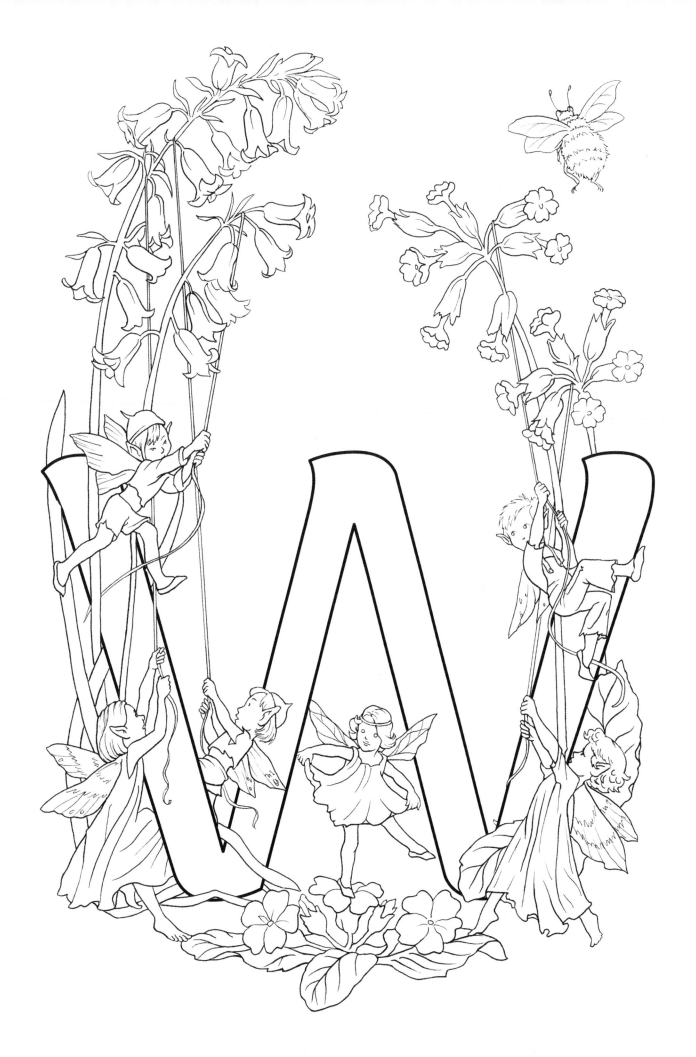

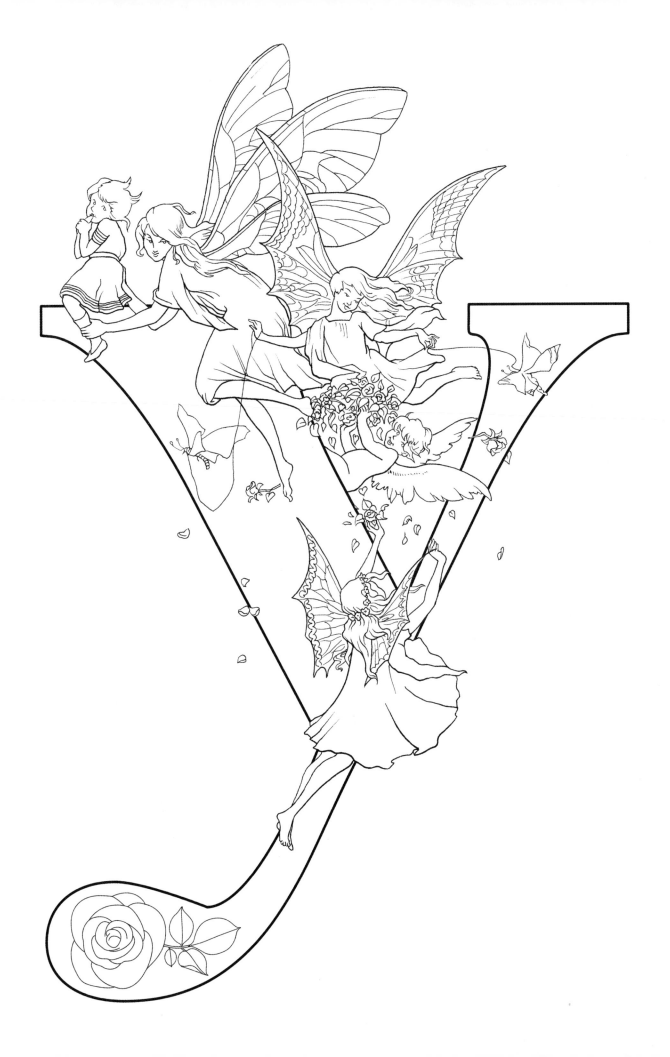

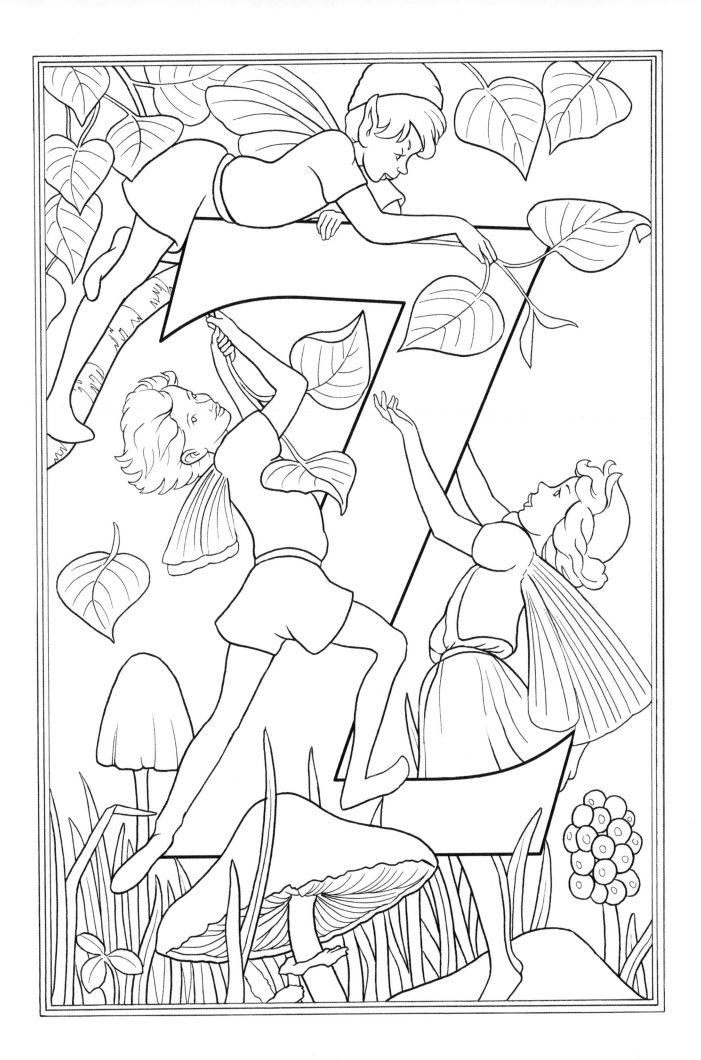

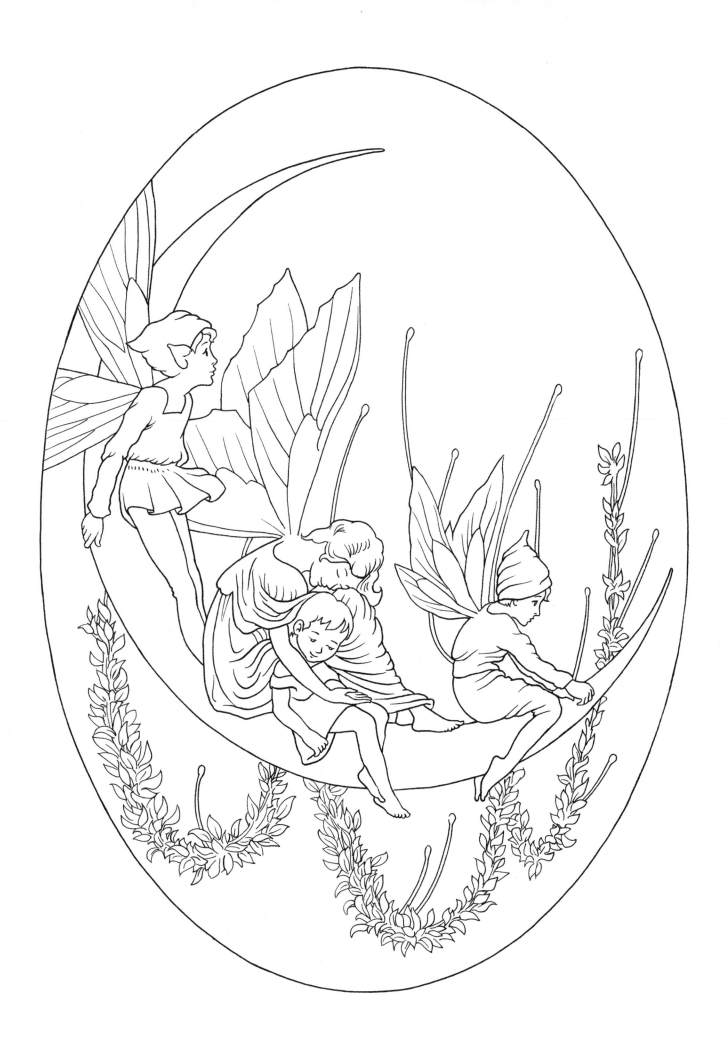